"Jim Bourey has accomplished the difficult task of presenting complex and sometimes technical detail on a wide variety of subjects in a very readable, easily understandable manner. He doesn't talk down to the reader, but writes with a personable manner in this very rewarding read. There is very little available on current subject of city/county management issues that is so complete or presented in such a straight-forward, practical manner as in this book. Bourey obviously has a great deal of experience in the subject material, and clearly and successfully shares his deep knowledge with his audience. While this work will appeal to practicing managers of all levels of experience, it should be required reading for students majoring in public administration, political science, planning, social services, policing, and other fields related to local government services. It fits well for any student from university to graduate school and would help prepare them for the local government management profession."

Thomas Hutka

A Guidebook for City and County Managers

Whether you are a student preparing for a career in public administration, a mid-career professional manager or a seasoned veteran, *A Guidebook for City and County Managers* provides policy guidance and advice to local governmental challenges and issues.

Assuming a knowledge of the basics of public management, James M. Bourey provides real-world recommendations for issues managers are facing this decade and beyond. Relying on experience from his long career in local government in chief executive positions in city, county and regional council management in locations throughout the United States, Bourey outlines the best approaches to the most critical issues for local governments. The book is comprehensive in its breadth of subject matter yet targeted in the recommendations that focus on the most critical issues. Social equity, environmental protection and global warming, good fiscal management, adequate public infrastructure and active citizen engagement are important themes throughout.

Merely being an administrative caretaker is not sufficient; managers must have the knowledge of ways to improve their communities and take the initiative to enhance the quality of life of its residents. Making a difference is both the reason for the job and its reward. This book helps provide a roadmap for the journey.

James M. Bourey works as an author and part-time consultant on local government management through his firm, Bourey Consulting. For most of his 43-year career, Bourey served as a local government manager, working in chief executive positions in city, county and regional council management in locations throughout the United States. He also worked in the private sector as the Director of Corporate Development for Elliott Davis and Director of Management Services with McGill Associates. Jim's management career includes serving as the County Administrator for Hennepin County, Minnesota (Minneapolis), and City Manager for Newport News, Virginia, and Greenville, South Carolina. He held a variety of other local government management positions in Seattle, Washington; Phoenix, Arizona; Tampa, Florida; and Tulsa, Oklahoma. Jim has developed over 20 annual budgets, some exceeding one billion dollars and has been the chief executive in organizations with as many as 10,000 employees.

Routledge Research in Public Administration and Public Policy

Affirmative Action in Malaysia and South Africa
Preference for Parity
Hwok-Aun Lee

Critical Perspectives on Public Systems Management in India
Through the Lens of District Administration
Amar K J R Nayak and Ram Kumar Kakani

Policy Making and Southern Distinctiveness
John C. Morris, Martin K. Mayer, Robert C. Kenter & R. Bruce Anderson

The Effects of Technology and Institutions on E-Participation
A Cross-National Analysis
Pragati Rawat & John C. Morris

A Guidebook for City and County Managers
Meeting Today's Challenges
James M. Bourey

Modern Weights and Measures Regulation in the United States
A Brief History
Craig A. Leisy

COVID-19 Pandemic, Public Policy and Institutions in India
Issues of Labour, Income, and Human Development
Edited by Indranil De, Soumyadip Chattopadhyay, Hippu Salk Kristle Nathan, and Kingshuk Sarkar

For more information about this series, please visit: www.routledge.com/Routledge-Research-in-Public-Administration-and-Public-Policy/book-series/RRPAPP

A Guidebook for City and County Managers
Meeting Today's Challenges

James M. Bourey

Routledge
Taylor & Francis Group

NEW YORK AND LONDON

First published 2022
by Routledge
605 Third Avenue, New York, NY 10158

and by Routledge
4 Park Square, Milton Park, Abingdon, Oxon, OX14 4RN

Routledge is an imprint of the Taylor & Francis Group, an informa business

© 2022 James M. Bourey

Library of Congress Cataloging-in-Publication Data
A catalog record for this title has been requested

ISBN: 978-1-03-219798-2 (hbk)
ISBN: 978-1-03-220224-2 (pbk)
ISBN: 978-1-00-326275-6 (ebk)

DOI: 10.4324/9781003262756

Typeset in Times New Roman
by Newgen Publishing UK

This book is dedicated to my wife, Ann, who has been my constant companion and partner for the past 44 years since we met. Throughout our 43 years of marriage, she has supported my professional and personal life in a way that everyone dreams for a life partner. That has included some very challenging times with work and through a few significant health issues. She has also provided wonderful support in my writing each of my two books. Neither this book nor my career would have been possible without her love and support.

Contents

Figures

Introduction

Managing cities and counties has never been an easy task, and many may very well argue that it is even harder in this century and, particularly, in this decade. Tough issues involving land use and transportation, water, sewer, stormwater and solid waste have been around for decades as have social service challenges. But the very difficult issues involving significant socio-economic disparities, racial prejudice and the police use of excessive force that have been too long in the background must be addressed. Additionally, the rising lack of civility and the proliferation of social media and widespread misinformation have made the job of city and county leaders that much more difficult.

In my previous book, *A Journey of Challenge, Commitment and Reward: Tales of a City/County Manager*, I invited local government managers to engage with me in my journey and the lessons I learned as a professional manager of cities and counties. In this book, I ask managers to allow me to join **their** journey managing local governments in this decade and beyond, allow me to join them by providing an in-depth view into a wide variety of important and often difficult issues they face and offer recommendations for addressing these challenges. While my first book served as a coaching tool for how managers are motivated, trained and effectively do their jobs, this book is about the substance of what managers do and hopefully will be a coaching tool for the critical recommendations they make.

This book will examine all the major areas of local government responsibility, tackle many of the most important and vexing problems in each of them and detail approaches and strategies for handling these issues. It provides a perspective on appropriate and effective actions that can be taken and advice to give elected officials. While my 43 years of managing cities, counties and a regional council of governments as well as serving as a consultant to local governments in many locations throughout the United States have provided many important insights,

DOI: 10.4324/9781003262756-1

I do not profess to have all the answers. And while I also rely on recent past and current literature on best practices, this will not be a guide to all the issues cities and counties face or be a one-stop guide for policy setting. This book deals in a meaningful way with the most important issues. My experience enables me to provide some recommendations to carefully consider in addressing the many challenges managers face. But this book is not focused directly on my experience but rather on addressing the issues that cities and counties face today. You will see that some of the issues included are not those that you would necessarily find in a traditional public policy text but may be most helpful for the practicing professional.

This book, as well as my first, was written to continue to contribute to the local government management profession to which I have dedicated most of my life. While it is written to assist all those leading any form of local government, it is primarily focused on those managing cities and counties in a council–manager form. As its predecessor, this book often uses stories of real situations to help illustrate a point and demonstrate the value of the recommended approach. Also, as with my earlier book, not everyone will agree with the perspective provided or the recommendations. However, this book will, hopefully, further the dialog and insight into tackling many thorny issues.

As someone who no longer works directly for the local government, I do have more latitude to express opinions about the current state of city and county council actions and decision-making. I promise not to take too much liberty with this newfound freedom and will fully respect the constraints managers are under.

Inherent values

Up-front, in this introduction, I need to fully disclose some values that are inherent in the perspective and recommendations that are included in this book. I believe that in one way or another, these are values that most of the readers will share. However, it is still important to be transparent about my perspective. So the following is a description of those values.

Natural environment

Preserving and restoring our natural environment is critical to our existence. The reality of global warming is totally apparent, and the collective damage we have done to the environment needs to be reversed.

Preserving and restoring natural areas as well as plant and animal species is also vital to our well-being.

Social justice

Promoting social justice includes doing what we can to ensure an equal opportunity and treatment for everyone as well as taking actions to correct for past unequal treatment. This must include action to eliminate the socio-economic disparities that have resulted from past discrimination.

Fairness

As we evaluate actions and recommendations, we need to always ask if it is fair to all concerned. Rotarians will certainly recognize that concept as part of the "Four Way Test." I was proud to be a Rotarian for many years.

Service

To local government managers, this is our mantra. We are all about providing service to our community. Again, the motto of Rotarians of "service above self" is totally fitting.

Kindness

Yes, I hold to the tenet that we need a kinder and gentler world. The level of animosity that we see so evidenced today is a significant threat to our civilized society.

Truth

The level of misinformation and outright falsehoods in the information streams in our country and the entire world are very scary. It is vital that we are not only always truthful but also promote true and correct information.

Diversity/Inclusion

While diversity and inclusion can be seen as part of social justice, I wanted to specifically call it out to be ever mindful that we must be diligent to ensure that our actions embrace diversity and are inclusionary for all people regardless of race, ethnicity or sexual orientation.

Trust

While many find it hard to do, we must innately trust others and work to gain their trust. I know that I have personally been disappointed and even wronged by people I have trusted but I still believe it is better to trust people implicitly rather than make everyone earn your trust. This does not mean being blind to others' actions but rather not always be suspicious of everyone. Likewise, we need to understand that it does not take much to damage the trust people have in us.

Transparency

Just as being transparent will help people trust you, the transparency in city operations will help to build the public trust in their local government.

Impartiality

While we all have our biases, we must strive to be as impartial in our actions as possible. It helps if we surround ourselves with people who not only have different perspectives but are also willing to challenge us and our perspectives.

Respect for others

Respecting others comes in so many forms, from simple daily actions to major decisions we make. Sometimes we can be seen as not respectful when it was not at all our intention. Therefore, we need to always work to demonstrate the respect that others deserve.

Empowerment

While much has been written about empowering employees, it is easy to fall into a trap of constraining people rather than empowering. This can come from what one may feel is an altruistic step to try to prevent someone from taking a misstep. If we do that often enough, employees will have no room to grow and be successful.

Personal responsibility

Taking responsibility for one's personal actions is essential for any manager and goes along with building trust, being transparent and being truthful.

Collaboration

We all know that things get done as a result of teams working together. Acting in a collaborative fashion is essential for the success of teams.

Community

All managers must care deeply about the community in which they work, but they also must value the community, that sense of being part of a place that shares some common interests, goals and aspirations.

Innovation

One of the most dreaded phrases a manager hates to hear when asking about why something was done in a certain manner is, "Because we have always done it that way!" Of course, being innovative goes well beyond the mundane and can be incredibly valuable for a community and other local governments as well.

Doing what is right

When it comes down to any decision, even those with many competing constituencies and implications for the manager, doing what is right is always the best guide.

I know that is a long list and a lot to take in, but I feel quite confident that there will not be a lot of disagreement with these values. You may feel that I have even left one out, but I think you get the idea of the perspective in this book.

Along with these values, there are certain beliefs that are important throughout the book. Decisions and recommendations need to be fact based and not based on misguided, unsubstantiated beliefs or ideas. This book is a reflective of state-of-the-art local government management practices. It builds on what we know and what we expect is coming in the near future. There is a particular sense of urgency to address two of the most critical issues of our time: achieving socio-economic equity and dramatically reducing global warming. There is also a belief that local government is the closest to the people and has the best opportunity to build the level of public trust. In addition, since most city and county issues are not inherently Democrat or Republican issues, local governments have the best chance of bringing down the level of divisiveness in the country and bringing about more harmony than what exists today.

Roles of the manager and council

While it is the council that is responsible for setting policy in a council–manager form of government, to be effective it needs to be done in conjunction with the city/county manager. At times, council members do initiate policies, but it is more often the manager who brings forward issues for the council to consider. Managers most often identify issues that need council actions. They almost always do analysis of a policy issue, look at alternative approaches, analyze those approaches and make a recommendation to the council. Managers will often check in with council members and discuss their alternatives as their work proceeds, sometimes testing some of their assumptions.

It is the council's responsibility to become informed on issues, suggest alternative approaches and give feedback to the manager as well as use their best judgment in making decisions on policies.

Organization of the book

This book is organized by thematic and functional areas of cities and counties, not by the typical departments. In each of these areas, the most important and difficult issues are discussed, and a perspective is provided including how best to address the issues. There is some natural overlap in the areas, but the issues are placed where the most important emphasis needs to be. Below are the areas that form the next 14 chapters of this book.

Social justice involves those points of focus that relate to combating systemic racism and providing an equal playing field for all residents in a community as well as those who would like to live there. It covers functional areas of local government services that have a major impact on social justice although other chapters also espouse positions that promote social justice.

Financing local government covers long-range financial planning, budgeting, taxes and fees as well as the funding of nonprofits.

Land use planning and controls include general land use patterns, growth management as well as land planning and controls.

Environmental stewardship encompasses the concepts of sustainability, resiliency, global warming and pollution as well as preservation.

Housing deals with the challenges of affordable housing, neighborhood revitalization/gentrification and homelessness.

Transportation includes transportation planning, different modes of transportation, funding and operations.

Public facilities/infrastructure covers water, wastewater, stormwater, solid waste and parks and recreation as well as the critical link with land use development.

Economic development involves an investigation of public incentives, public investment, job creation, marketing and economic impact studies.

Education focuses on those issues that are often the purview of cities or counties such as funding and capital projects as well as the role in promoting and supporting educational institutions and training programs.

Health care is limited to those roles generally provided by local governments although that does extend to operating public hospitals. It includes public health and employee wellness.

Intergovernmental relations focus on federal and state regulations, federal and state funding for local governments, lobbying and regional governance.

Technology encompasses local government automation, community Wi-Fi and broadband as well as budgeting for technology

Citizen engagement/Transparency are combined because they go hand in hand with one another. This chapter covers informing citizens and being transparent, engaging citizens in meetings and getting input on projects and dealing with incivility.

The final chapter, **Conclusion**, will bring the points into additional focus for what it all means for governing cities and counties.

1 Social justice

In this decade and beyond, I believe that achieving social justice in our communities will be our greatest challenge. Centuries of prejudice, repression and unequal treatment have resulted in extensive socio-economic disparities that have further reinforced unequal treatment and made it even harder for the repressed to obtain the benefits of our modern society. While the excessive use of force by police officers has been an ongoing problem for decades, it came to a head in 2020 as high-profile abuses resulted in the deaths of African Americans. It has been encouraging that a majority of Americans recognize the need to address this discriminatory behavior.

Of course, efforts to promote social justice are not new. One of my favorite books from graduate school was entitled *Social Justice and the City*. Written by David Harvey, it was originally published almost 50 years ago. It was republished in 2009. In this seminal work, Harvey examines the relationship of the geography of cities and their planning to the socio-economic characteristics of residents and the challenges presented to social equity. From this work, it is clear that many of the hurdles must be overcome to help provide for social justice. While we have made some progress in our country in the past five decades, I would argue that we are certainly closer to the starting point than we are to achieving a goal of social justice.

Dictionary.com defines social justice as the "fair treatment of all people in a society, including respect for the rights of minorities and equitable distribution of resources among members of a community" (Dictionary.com n.d.). In their public administration program, Kent State University (KSU) outlines five principles of social justice (KSU, Public Administration n.d.):

- Access to resources
- Equity

DOI: 10.4324/9781003262756-2

- Diversity
- Participation
- Human rights

I will use the above definition and principles as the general framework in this chapter and elsewhere in this book where social justice is referenced.

When one examines the values I have outlined in the Introduction, it is fairly obvious why a socially just community is critically important. At the same time, while I strongly advocate for local government managers to push for social justice, they cannot, by themselves, make their communities more socially just. It will take the broader community as well as action at a state and national level.

Despite the challenge for managers to improve social justice, their work can make a huge difference for communities and the approaches to the major issues outlined in this chapter can substantially move the needle. In fact, all recommendations that managers make need to be examined through the lens of whether or not it promotes social justice.

While the five principles of social justice can help guide decision-making, we need a more definitive strategy for obtaining socially just communities. Not only do we need to live by these principles, but we must also attack the roots of the socio-economic disparities that hold people back from achieving an equal access to resources. The idea of paying reparations for effects of sins of the past, including slavery and repressive laws, is being discussed in many communities. Instead of approaching reparations as a financial payment, it needs to be considered as the basis for an expanded investment in reversing the causes of socio-economic disparity. By making this investment, we can give people the opportunity to obtain equal access to resources to obtain the housing, food and all the attributes of a comfortable life. The best analogy is the quote you have likely heard that is attributed to Confucius, "Give a man a fish and you'll feed him for the day. Teach a man to fish, and you've feed him for a lifetime."

This chapter includes a framework aimed at reducing racial prejudice and socio-economic disparities. This framework was originally described in an article in ICMA's *PM* magazine that I coauthored with Richard Myers, the former Newport News Police Chief, with whom I worked when I was the city manager. This article, entitled *Innovations in Addressing Racism and Police Excessive Use of Force* (Bourey and Myers 2020, 39–43), described the framework, which encompassed the following:

- An extensive community engagement program
- A program of criminal justice reform
- Police department operational changes
- Education and job training
- Social services support

In addition to attacking racial prejudice and systemic discrimination, this framework is based on the premise that it is only when those who have been repressed are given skills and support to effectively participate in our modern socio-economic system then we will eliminate the effects of centuries of discrimination. While ongoing efforts to improve neighborhood conditions of those who have been subject to discrimination are important and should be continued, communities need to prioritize their investment directly in the socio-economically deprived. The deteriorated physical surroundings can be improved, but its residents will not achieve equal access to resources without enhancing their skills to be successful in the modern world. This chapter will include a description of the programmatic recommendations necessary to reverse prejudice and build the underpinnings for success.

Before describing each of these critical elements in the framework, I want to focus on recommendations for the social service system operation. While I spent a lot of my career with cities and being responsible for all those typical city services, I did spend a good amount of time leading county operations, and in Virginia, the cities also provide all the services for a community including those typically provided by counties. Nowhere was I more challenged with the delivery of social services more than when I was the Hennepin County Administrator. Hennepin County includes the City of Minneapolis and 45 other cities and had about a quarter of the state's population. Approximately 75% of the 10,000 staff members and well over one billion dollar budget was devoted to human services. This included managing all the social services as the state delegated that to the counties, including economic assistance, children and family services and mental health. It also included a post-sentencing incarceration facility and parole officers as well as a teaching hospital licensed for 1,000 beds (about 500 in operation at the time) with a large staff of doctors and a health maintenance organization insuring 100,000 lives.

Upon assuming my responsibilities, it became evident that the various departments were operating quite independently despite having many clients in common. People bounced from one agency to another, and no one was looking after their overall well-being. When people went to different agencies, they needed to supply the very same basic information every time. The county also partnered with 600 social service providers, all serving the same clients. I find this analogous to the circumstances in which I found my mother after my dad passed away and my wife and I became engaged with her care due to her Alzheimer's diagnosis. She was on 13 different medications prescribed by a few different doctors. Some medications inhibited the actions of others. We took her to a primary care physician who was able to view all her medications, their interactions and her real needs and dramatically reduce the number of drugs she took.

In the same way, Hennepin County sought to look at the clients from a holistic perspective. If we could share data across our organizations, it would help us to get much closer to this reality. At the time, which is still true today to some extent, there were strong prohibitions on sharing information from one program to another in order to protect the confidentially of the individual. We did make progress but did not achieve the full integration of data we would like to have achieved. We wanted to take a caseworker approach with someone looking after the entire well-being of the client. This is still the model that we need to use in approaching our social service system.

Community engagement program

Most people would undoubtedly say that eliminating racial bias and the discrimination against people for other reasons such as ethnicity or sexual orientation is a truly audacious goal. It is indeed an audacious goal. But it is a hill we must climb. Local government leaders can and must lead the charge up that steep slope. Is it something we can totally attain in our lifetimes? Probably not. However, we can make a huge difference in the battle to erase discrimination. It will take a huge commitment of time and resources to make the needed progress. We simply must make that commitment of our time and resources.

We need a galvanized effort at the federal, state and local level. City and county leaders need to advocate for this resource allocation at those higher levels. They also need to commit the needed funding and staff time at the local level and press for the local business community to do the same. In the *PM* article referenced previously, Rick and I describe the approach at the local level in the following way (Bourey and Myers 2020, 39):

> An extensive and robust community engagement approach is vital to address explicit and implicit racial bias. This must be a joint effort of public and private city leaders and professionals to engage

the entire community in order to educate the community about racial bias and win over the hearts and minds of residents. This will require difficult conversations that must take place. Communities will need to take advantage of all means of communicating with citizens, including social media, and diversity trainers and community involvement professionals can design engagement strategies to help guide the efforts. This will not be a quick process and communities need to be willing to see it through to make the meaningful difference that is essential to address racial bias. Certainly not everyone's views will be changed. However, if the overwhelming majority of residents better understand racial bias and are committed to accepting, respecting, and celebrating one another's differences, the dynamic will be very different than it is today in many places.

This will need to be a multi-year effort and, in fact, will always need to be a community priority. It will also require an annual major commitment of resources.

The first order of business needs to be gaining the buy-in of local public and private sector businesses and bringing them through an intense training series to sensitize them to the dynamics, issues and results of racial bias and other discriminations. There are models that exist for this type of program. One that I am familiar with and have participated in is the Diversity Leaders Initiative, a program of Furman University's Riley Institute. The Riley Institute is named after Richard Riley who served as the Governor of South Carolina and the Secretary of Education under President Bill Clinton. This program began in 2003 in the Upstate South Carolina area (generally, around Greenville) and has subsequently been expanded to the Midlands (Columbia) and Low Country (Charleston) areas. Thus far, there have been more than 2,300 high-level community leaders who have participated in the program. Each class has approximately 40 participants who take part in an interactive learning and development experience around diversity. The program has won many awards and has made an appreciable difference in the understanding of diversity and commitment to equal treatment of all people in their communities. As a follow-up to these programs, there is an annual get-together called *One South Carolina* attended by past program participants where there is an update on the progress of the classes as well as a commitment to certain additional actions to promote diversity inclusion and equality.

While not everyone will be able to participate in this type of rigorous program, the community leaders who have gone through this program will be critically important in the effort to reach out to a broad section of the city. An outreach program to connect with the general population will need to be designed by local leaders and professional experts in engaging a community. This outreach will need to involve all types of media, including social media. While no one can be compelled to participate, the idea is to encourage a broad spectrum of the community to be engaged. In addition to community leaders, well-known personalities such as prosports and entertainment personalities can be tremendously important for bringing the message to most people in the community. It has been very encouraging to see so many in the world of professional sports show a commitment to making a difference in racial and ethnic equality. Of course, not everyone will be receptive to the message, but if we can change the hearts and minds of enough people such that a majority of people evidence a commitment to antidiscrimination, they can help to mute the actions of those who do not.

While pursuing this community engagement program, the local government needs to lead the way in creating and supporting a diverse work force free of discrimination. They need to do extensive training in racial bias and cultural awareness. In addition, the hiring and promotion process must contain a strong commitment and procedures that result in a diverse staff, especially at the higher levels of management. One of the key issues in such a program is to work hard for a broad applicant pool. Additionally, it will be important to look carefully within the organization for people who may have been overlooked. I have found this to be particularly helpful and have found some real superstars who had not been previously identified. In my first book, I related a particular situation when I was the Hennepin County, Minnesota, administrator where I elevated someone two levels to a department director level. Dr David Sanders was a true superstar who went on to lead the largest children and family services department in the country. Managers must not just wait for people to apply but have an active recruitment program.

Criminal justice reform

While the criminal justice system has been studied for rules, regulations and actions that are discriminatory, there has not been a lot of change and most of the emphasis has been on policing. However, every step in the criminal justice system from arraignment to bail to court procedures to sentencing to parole needs to be reviewed and scrubbed to eliminate innate bias.

One of the major issues that need particular attention is the concept of qualified immunity. Qualified immunity is a principal that provides an employee or appointed official immunity from civil lawsuits as long as the individual does not violate a statutory or constitutional right that should have been evident to them. This applies to all governmental officials, including police officers. Given the nature of their work, the doctrine has had particular importance for police officers. Some think that this has shielded them from holding them accountable for inappropriate actions and needs to be modified or taken away. I cannot advocate for changing this doctrine because if someone's constitutional rights are violated and a reasonable person would have known they were being violated, the officer does not have immunity. I do not believe that eliminating this principal would assist in holding officers accountable.

Police operational changes

There indeed has been a lot of study as well as reports on changes that need to be made in the operation of police departments and the rules and regulations that affect police departments. Advocates of reform have sometimes pushed for a "defunding of police," by which they mean reducing police department budgets. A simple defunding of police would accomplish little and could even put the public's safety at risk. There are instances where a shift in resources from the police department to other departments which can fulfill a role instead of the police may offer some benefit.

Reforms that would reduce racially biased actions and the excessive use of force include the following:

Reform the hiring process

We need to look for police officers with a different set of skills than has historically been required. Police officers must have good interpersonal skills that will enable them to interact with a wide variety of people. They must have high ethical standards and they cannot have a racial bias. The methods used to evaluate candidates need to screen officers for these qualities and only select officers who have these qualities. Additionally, there needs to be a greater diversity among the officers hired so that the police force is reflective of the community.

Revise police officer training

Police academy training as well as the field training officer experience need to be overhauled. Officers need to develop their skills in engaging with the full diversity of people that exists in the community. They need to develop their skill in deescalating situations. It is also critically important that they be indoctrinated in the appropriate use of force and understand that use of excessive force will not be tolerated. They also need to be fully educated in the concept and practice of community-oriented policing. While steps need to be taken to involve professionals skilled in handling mentally ill people, officers will generally most often be the first on the scene. They need to have some skill set in handling the situations involving people with mental issues, at least until expert help can arrive. This is especially true when the person may have some type of weapon they may use on another or themselves.

Develop a new system of evaluating officers

Evaluation systems for police officers as well as the command staff need to reflect how well they engage in community policing and emulate the desired conduct of an officer that they learned in the police academy. Productivity statistics should be de-emphasized in favor of information about the way an officer does their job.

Revamp the procedures for disciplining and dismissing police officers

Constraints on disciplining and dismissing officers is currently an impediment to police department management's ability to correct racially biased behavior and an excessive use of force. The pendulum has swung way over to the side of protecting officers from actions, resulting in the inability to correct problems and fire officers for clearly racially biased actions or an unacceptable use of force. While police unions may have provided positive benefits at some time, their frequent blind defense of offending officers is counterproductive. Union contracts will need to be changed, as will state laws governing personnel procedures.

Share information across jurisdictions of police officer misconduct

Even when police departments dismissed officers, it too often leads to those officers moving on to another department and committing the same offenses. There needs to be a sharing of information across all police departments about the inappropriate behavior of an officer in any department they worked. I realize this flies in the face of the current common practice of local government employers not sharing any information about a former employee except the dates of their employment. This must change for police officers.

Revisit the kinds of services and calls to which the police respond

While police can and need to be trained to handle a wide variety of situations, they will never be as skilled as professionals trained to handle people such as the mentally ill. We often expect too much of our officers and need to examine carefully what we ask them to do. We need to look at the type of calls they respond to and use others to provide needed services. This would include situations such as domestic violence. Having a social worker investigate domestic violence incidence along with a police officer can significantly improve the outcome.

Reinforce evidence-based policing

Police department policies need to reflect proven best practices and standards established by professional organizations such as the Commission on Accreditation for Law Enforcement Agencies (CALEA). In fact, every city or county police or sheriff's department should go through the accreditation process.

Operate on a true community-based policing model

The concept of community policing has been around for many years. Indeed, a large number of departments throughout the country say that they follow a community-based policing model. This was certainly the case when I assumed the position of City Manager for the City of Newport News, Virginia. However, this was far from the case. The notion of community-based policing at that time was to go to some community meetings. The officers rarely got out of their vehicles. I likened it more to drive by policing. The officers not only did not regularly engage with members of the community, but many officers did not know how to engage. Earlier I mentioned the police chief I hired, Richard Myers. He needed to become personally engaged to help the training process of teaching officers how to engage with people in the community, particularly in the predominately Black neighborhoods. He also needed to get the officers out of their vehicles to be in more personal contact with residents.

Community policing is all about engaging with people on their turf, in nonthreatening ways and building a level of rapport with children and adults. You know you have made good progress when people in a given neighborhood say, the officer X is "their" policeman.

Education and job training

While a future chapter is dedicated to education, there are some key things that need to be covered in this chapter that are critical to the specific effort of enabling those who have been repressed due to discrimination to be successful in obtaining an equal footing. A good education is the underpinning of future successful employment. Community support for education from preschool through high school is vital and will be discussed in later chapters.

Educators know that effective schools are only part of the answer to a good education. Adult support and encouragement are also vital. Children in disadvantaged backgrounds often do not have the parental support that benefit others. So mentoring programs that help provide that support are important and necessary.

As important as traditional education is, it is also vital that children in disadvantaged situations learn the life skills important for success in a modern world. This includes a knowledge of what employers are going to want from their employees, financial literacy and ability to understand and cope with the challenges a complicated world will present to them. The Achievable Dream Academies offer a great example of schools that offer that critical life skill development. Originating in Newport News, Achievable Dream Academies are now operating in Virginia Beach and Richmond. They teach the life skills such as handling financial transactions.

In addition to all the tangible skills that the Achievable Dream Academies provide, they also assist in developing a sense of self-worth in students. So many children from underprivileged backgrounds who lack supportive parents see very little that is positive in their lives and do not have much hope for the future. Many see virtually no future at all. Too many kids when asked what they would like to do with their lives say that they have not really considered it because they do not expect to live long enough. The culture of violence is very real and deleterious for them. The sense of self-worth that is instilled in the students is as critical as anything else they acquire.

Each year, the schools have a black tie dinner and auction fund raiser. As part of that evening, the seniors who will be graduating that year walk into the banquet hall dressed in their cap and gowns. As they walk in with their heads held high and smiles on their faces, you can see that they know their lives matter. When you talk with them and look in their eyes, you know they can see a future. Making that kind of a difference in their lives is so very special.

Job training is a critical part of the educational support needed for those who do not end up pursuing a four-year degree. There needs to be increased investment in technical school programs that teach skills that will lead to employment in the community. Additionally, while the federal government provides some funds for job training programs, communities need to step up the funding and expand these programs to reach more people and needed skill sets. Cities also need to work with businesses to establish apprentice programs that directly lead to jobs.

Social services support

Many readers probably remember the slogan, "It takes a village to raise a child." Whether a village is required or not, the point is that children need a support system that will nurture them and promote their learning and growth into adulthood. Many children in disadvantaged homes do not have a home environment that provides them the necessary level of support to recognize their potential. Thus, some of the required support may need to come from "the village."

Cities and counties can help to ensure a nurturing environment by providing key services. This should include parenting classes to help fathers and mothers provide better care for their children. They can also encourage the development of youth mentoring programs. It is clear that having a responsible adult in their lives is vital to a child's development. It is also critical the local governments support quality childcare options that are affordable for those lower wage earners. With the high cost of day care, governmental subsidies are critical.

In addition to supporting children, alcohol and drug treatment is vital for many in the community to live successful lives. Unfortunately, that applies to children as well as adults. These programs need to be robust and affordable and be in place as an alternative to jail or prison. Many believe that the deinstitutionalization of mental health has helped to greatly exacerbate the homelessness of mentally ill people. We must turn that around and provide mental health services for those who have no resources to pay.

This obviously is critical for the challenges the police are experiencing with mental health crises that become a police issue. No matter how much the police get extra training to deal with mental health problems they encounter, they will never be skilled enough to address this issue like a mental health professional can.

Just as every individual needs to have sufficient financial means to support themselves, the finances of cities are also critically important. The next chapter provides an in-depth view of the financing of cities.

References

Bourey, James, and Myers, Richard. 2020. "Innovations in Addressing Racism and Police Excessive Use of Force." *PM* 102, No. 11 (November): 36–43.

Dictionary.com. "Social Justice." Accessed August 19, 2021. www.dictionary.com/brouse/social-justice.

Harvey, David. 1973. *Social Justice and the City*. Baltimore: Johns Hopkins University Press.

Kent State University, Public Administration. "The Five Principles of Social Justice." Accessed August 19, 2021. https://onlinedegrees.kent.edu/political-science/master-of-public-administration/community/five-principles-of-social-justice.

2 Local government finance

This chapter assumes that the reader knows the basics about financial management. It builds on the nuts and bolts of local government budgeting, focusing on some strategic approaches to local government finance that are important for managers. First, the approach to doing a five-year financial forecast will be described along with some benefits that these forecasts contain. Following this, there is a discussion of comparing the tax and fees for peer cities. Subsequently, the issue of impact/capacity fees is explored. Then an approach to enhancing revenue is described, followed by an exploration of other postretirement employee benefits (OPEB). Additionally, there is a perspective on approaching budget development, particularly in times of financial strain, and the need to substantially reduce costs and the importance of rating agency visits. Finally, a strategy for the funding of nonprofits is presented.

Five-year financial forecasts

It is encouraging that more and more cities are doing five-year financial forecasts but surprising that it has taken as long as it has for this trend to develop. I have been engaged in long-range financial planning for more than 25 years and have initiated this process in the past four organizations I have managed, which include a county, a regional organization and two cities. The value of these forecasts for developing a more strategic approach for the organization and especially for the actions of the council has been huge.

Local governments generally approach developing a five-year financial forecast in a similar fashion, but there are some important considerations that may not always be included. Both revenues and expenditures are usually projected using trend line information. This typically includes not only projected inflationary increases but also items such as employee salary increases and health care costs at a rate of projected

DOI: 10.4324/9781003262756-3

potential increase. It is important to examine other items you are relatively confident will occur to modify those trend lines. For instance, if you have an aggressive capital improvements program in the next few years, it would be beneficial to add the cost of staff that will be needed to operate the facilities that will be coming online during that time. This might also include instances like where a grant might have been used to add employees and the city will need to pick up added cost to maintain those employees. It is important that the long-range financial forecasts involve each of the departments as they will always be most knowledgeable about their programs and which budget pressures they will be facing in the next few years.

While virtually every place that does long-range forecasting includes the general fund, many do not focus on other funds as well. Including the other major funds such as the enterprise funds for sewer, water, stormwater and solid waste can be very helpful. It is also valuable to develop scenarios based on some different assumptions in order to gain a better sensitivity for what might have a significant effect on the budget. It is always good to look at what might happen with a major downturn in the economy and how that would affect the potential financial outcomes.

It is critical to develop a balanced budget scenario. The council needs to see ways that the revenue shortfalls can be met by additional revenues. By showing some different alternative approaches to funding deficits, the council can provide feedback on their most favored options. Additionally, it is important to help the media's perspective if they are reporting on the exercise. I painfully remember one year when faced with a newspaper headline about the huge deficit the city was facing.

Aside from just getting everyone focused more strategically, there are many benefits to doing a five-year forecast. It becomes an educational process for the council to better understand the budget. It helps the council to think about challenges the city faces a few years down the road and will encourage them to make decisions that are not stopgap measures and merely getting through just one year at a time. They will also be better able to see the long-term consequences of an annual budget decision. One example of this is that in instances with both the City of Greenville, South Carolina, and Newport News, Virginia, the councils went along with my recommendation that they assume that each year the city will make an inflationary adjustment to utility rates. The long-range forecast showed them that if they did not do this each year, they would be stuck with making a fairly large increase at some point, which would cause significant discontent with customers.

My experience has borne out the idea that the best time to do a long-range forecast and discuss it with the council is after the departments have had an opportunity to put their budgets together but before the manager has started to work through the departmental requests and make funding decisions. This gives the departments a better understanding of their needs and allows them to feed into the process and yet gives the council a chance to provide input on their priorities and views on revenues and expenditures. I have found that this timing and process has helped the council feel like they have had early input into the budget process and develop a level of confidence in the budget. I believe this is partly responsible for the fact that both in Greenville and Newport News, there were a few years when the councils did not change one penny of my recommended annual budget.

To illustrate some additional dimensions of long-range financial forecasting, I will describe a consulting project I was involved in during the 2019–20 time frame. In describing this project, I need to first point out the significant irony it was for me to be involved in this effort. I started my career working for the consolidated city and county of Metropolitan Nashville and Davidson County (Metro). I left this position 40 years before this engagement. Additionally, from 2010 to 2013, I worked for Elliott Davis, a southeast regional accounting firm, which included a consulting operation and an excellent local government practice. Fast forward to late 2019, I was approached by the leader of the public services practice of Elliott Davis to provide assistance with a potential consulting project for the Metropolitan Nashville Chamber of Commerce to study the Metropolitan Nashville Budget. So, I guess you can go home again!

Many in the Nashville business community were concerned that Metro was not keeping up with the demand for additional infrastructure and service demands. The State of Tennessee has a requirement that when local governments have a comprehensive property tax reassessment, they "roll back" the property tax rate such that no more revenue is collected than in the current year. However, the council can decide to raise that level and even set the tax rates the same as they were to take advantage of the increase in the assessments. Since much of the increase in assessments comes from new structures, which create additional service demands, it does make sense that at least some of the increase in property tax revenues be captured to pay for increasing demands. Additionally, since some of the increase in assessments is due to inflationary increases and the cost to operate also is subject to inflationary increases, there is another reason to capture some of the increased revenues. However, during the last comprehensive reassessment, Metro had rolled back the rate and not taken advantage of any of the increased revenues despite the fact that Nashville was growing relatively quickly, and its service needs were as well. Partially due to this rollback and partially due to an unwillingness to raise taxes for a number of years, many felt Metro was in a difficult financial position. The Chamber wanted an outside expert's view on the current Metro financial position and advice on what potential policy positions they should take related to its financial practices. While the contract was with the Chamber, the Nashville Board of Realtors provided funding for this project, and we were fully engaged with them as a partner as well.

The Chamber issued a request for proposal (RFP) for consulting services. Not only did Elliott Davis have an office in Nashville, but they also had significant involvement with the Chamber. I was asked to be involved because of my city/county management experience. I recommended that former city manager Gary Jackson, a colleague and friend, also be added to the team. In addition to being a city manager for decades, Gary had worked extensively in the City of Dallas budget office. In analyzing the RFP, I felt like there were two things that we should recommend as additions to the Chamber's proposed scope of work. This included a five-year financial forecast. In addition, they had asked for a comparison of the tax rates of similar peer cities. A comparison of the total tax and fee burden would be the best comparison as cities raise revenues in various ways and one can only compare the demands on residents to pay for city services by looking at the total picture. These two suggested additional services greatly assisted in their decision process.

We were indeed selected to do the work and completed the project over a few months period. As it turns out, the five-year financial projection was an absolute key to the project as it clearly demonstrated Metro's structurally unbalanced budget. It showed that without a significant increase in revenues, Metro would face larger and larger deficits each year. Based on our analysis, it was clear that the fact that Metro had not taken advantage of some of the revenue growth played a large role in the structural imbalance.

Peer city comparisons

Describing the approach to the peer city review is important for illustrating the best way to make valid comparisons. I am concerned about a heavy reliance on benchmarking one city with another. Regardless of the nature of the service, conditions vary so much from place to place that it makes benchmarking comparisons often misleading. For instance, comparing the cost to maintain roadways varies a great deal with the weather as well as with the street construction as well as the amount and type of traffic using the road.

Of course, the selection of cities to use can help make comparing cities more useful or less consequential. For the Nashville project, we sought cities/counties with similarities to Metro Nashville. This included the size of the area, whether it was a consolidated government, the general age of the development, whether it was a state capital and whether it was a growing entity. The six cities we used as a basis of comparison were Charlotte, Austin, Jacksonville, Louisville, Indianapolis and Denver.

As was mentioned earlier, we looked at the total tax and fee burden. In order to do this, we needed a basis of comparison so we could consider the total financial burden. We used a typical, average household in Nashville as the basis for the comparison. We documented the characteristics of the household, including the house price, household income, amount of utilities consumed and goods purchased. We then applied the various taxes and fees that this typical household would pay in Nashville and the six peer cities. The comparison clearly showed the very low tax and fee burden that Nashville had in relationship to each of the peer cities.

There were many other dimensions of the study such as OPEB costs, which were very high in Nashville, the transit system and affordable housing. The study was very well received and used by the Chamber and Board of Realtors in the development of their public policy recommendations. I believe it was also helpful for the Metro Council to see that they needed to take action to raise additional revenue. Of course, the coronavirus pandemic took hold before the budget was adopted and the revenues decreased significantly enough that a major property tax increase was absolutely necessary.

Enhancing revenue

This leads into a discussion of some suggestions on approaches to taxes and fees. It is a bit ironic that I played a part in a study that demonstrated the need for a property tax increase, since I have never included a property tax rate increase in the budgets I have recommended as a local government manager. Although I have not recommended a *rate increase*, I have always recommended keeping the tax rate in place when an increase in the property tax assessment base occurs. This is really for the same reasons as was evident in the Nashville study; as a city grows out and up and as inflation increases the cost of doing business, the city's demands for revenue will also increase. Yes, there are times when property assessment increases can outstrip inflation, but they are fairly rare, and that is a time to build up the community's reserves for when a recession hits. The recent experience of going through the COVID-19 virus pandemic served as a painful reminder to most managers of the need to maintain a healthy reserve fund.

Another reason why I have not recommended property tax rate increases is I have often pushed user fees to be sure to cover all their costs and not rely on a general fund subsidy. This has included water, wastewater, stormwater and solid waste. If a community does not have a stormwater fee, it is a good vehicle to use to assist in needed revenue growth, especially with the increasing demands for treating stormwater to improve the quality and reduce the quantity of urban runoff. That seems like a more equitable approach. It is often more acceptable to the governing body as well.

Another important way that communities can raise revenue without raising taxes is to implement a system of impact or capacity fees to help pay for public facilities. This topic warrants its own discussion.

Impact/capacity fees

Many, if not most, communities at one time or another have a debate about whether growth should "pay for itself." The entire notion of what "paying for itself" means has different interpretations. Managers who have been through this debate know that community tensions can run high on the topic and generally would classify this as a thorny issue. For the purpose of this discussion, we will focus on growth paying for itself as the developers paying for the proportion of the public facilities will be used by those living or working in the development. The idea of growth paying for itself often also includes the long-term operating cost compared to the taxes and fees generated by the development. Any attempt to answer this broad-level question of whether growth is paying for itself in a community is a very complex endeavor that is beyond the scope of this book.

A developer's upfront payment to help fund facilities that would be required by a development have generally been referred to as impact fees but have also been called capacity fees when they are used to defray costs for utility infrastructure like water and wastewater systems. State laws govern how these fees can be charged. For instance, in North Carolina, the fees for water and wastewater, referred to as system development fees, are controlled by a law guiding the amount of the charge based on the size of the development and a detailed study required in order to adopt and levy the fees. Impact fees have been instituted to cover a wide range of facilities. These include not only water and wastewater that have been mentioned but also stormwater, parks and recreation, transportation, police and fire and libraries.

While arguments can be made to charge fees for any of the mentioned services, if state laws allow, the best approach is to levy fees for the hard infrastructure including water, wastewater, stormwater and transportation. The impact of development on these types of services can be reasonably quantified.

Figuring the amount to charge can be a challenge, but there are methodologies that yield solid justifications. The North Carolina methodology specified in House Bill 436 provides some excellent guidance that is broadly applicable for water and wastewater charges. In order to charge fees in North Carolina, the jurisdiction must conduct a definitive study. Setting the charges for transportation really requires a detailed knowledge of transportation planning. While there are standard trip generation rates that assign a certain number of trips for various types of land uses, translating the impact the development will have on the road and transit network is complex.

In setting impact or capacity fees, the city must consider what the local market will bear for the fees. The city must know that the fees charged by developers will certainly be passed along to the renter or buyer of the properties. This can especially be counterproductive for communities trying to increase the supply of affordable housing. Cities also must recognize that these fees should be restricted to paying for the capital cost of facilities, as the properties will generate taxes and utility fees that contribute to the cost of operations.

Other postretirement employee benefits

Yet another sticky issue for cities and counties is benefits for retired employees. Most often, local governments have limited flexibility in determining the retirement payments, which are generally determined by the state if they are participating in a state system. It is more often that they have some flexibility in setting the OPEB for retirees. It is quite evident that these postretirement benefits can pose a large financial burden on the municipality. This is largely driven by health plan benefits, some of which have consisted of very rich plans offering great benefit for the retiree. Most jurisdictions have dialed back these benefits in one way or another.

There are three strategies that can be pursued to help reduce the long-term financial liability for the city. First is to stop paying the premium or any part of the premium of a health insurance policy for retirees and rather provide an amount of money that the employee can use to pay for a premium whether it is the city's plan or one they get on the open market. Second is to drop retirees from a city plan when they reach 65 years of age and are eligible for Medicare and then just provide a dollar amount for the retiree to purchase a supplemental policy. Last, work to reduce the amount of subsidy for employees who are not yet retired or at the least have not vested in the retirement system.

Budget development strategy

Most managers have experienced the phenomena of a council spending more time and debate on some of the smaller items in a proposed budget. They also may have experienced a council really getting into the weeds and nitpicking at departmental budgets. I believe that there are two principal reasons for this happening. First, many council members are not comfortable dealing with the large revenue and expense numbers in many budgets. It is not part of their experience and is hard for them to grasp how to address potential changes. They are more comfortable with some of the smaller line items that relate more to their personal budgets or some items in their work. This focus on smaller budget items also can be a way to feel like they are making a difference and contributing to improving the budget.

Council members are more effective when they can grasp the big picture and focus on the major components of the budget that will make a significant difference. It is up to the manager to help the council understand and be engaged at a strategic level. Unfortunately, I have seen some managers intentionally attempt to keep the council away from the major issues and away from dealing with significant issues. The manager before me in one of the localities I managed prided himself in putting together a detailed budget without the board's input and serving it up to them in volumes of paper without a good overview such that they needed to sort through to find out what was in it. Managers like this want control and not have the council "interfere" with them. Of course, they have that backwards; that it is really the council's responsibility. In order to deliver a budget that has the council's imprint and influence, it is incumbent on the manager to help the council be engaged in the strategy of developing the budget. The value of a five-year financial plan in doing this was described earlier.

Any manager who has been around long enough has had the unenviable task of preparing a budget in very lean years where reducing funding levels is required. This section will not provide a step-by-step guide through this process but rather will describe a general approach that I have found most helpful in this process. Facing a very tight year, it is essential to have as clear a picture as possible on the expected level of revenues. Using the best assumptions available, I have worked with the city's fiscal experts to predict the amount of expenditures that can be supported. This information led to establishing a target for the various departments in preparing their budgets. Each department was then asked to prepare a budget based on a percentage of the revenue they have in the current year. This level was set somewhat less than the ultimate budget would allow. For instance, I used 95% of the revenue in several instances.

The departments were expected to produce a budget with this level of funding that would support their entire operation. In many instances, faced with this challenge, departments have found ways to provide for the current level of service delivery through greater efficiencies. However, it has also been the case that some have found that they cannot deliver the same services for the reduced amount. In anticipation of this, they were also asked to list items that they would want to add back to the budget if more money were available. The departments were requested to present these "budget enhancements" in priority order for consideration in the process. These budget enhancements were configured as a program that they would add back to restore a program that they had to cut or add one they felt was necessary. As we worked through the budget, we added back items that we felt were the highest priority for the citizens and the council.

Two things are different from the way some approach preparing a reduced budget. First, this does not result in an across-the-board cut to each department. Frankly, across-the-board cuts are an easy way out for the manager and do not necessarily reflect the priorities of the council or community. All departments will not have an equal ability to cut costs or cut services that may not be as essential.

Second, it makes a difference whether you ask departments to cut 5% or to prepare a budget with 5% less funding. That may sound like semantics, but there is a different mindset in the two approaches. If they are challenged to prepare a full budget that may be all they get, it will come out differently from if they prepare a budget with the same amount of funds and just identify things to cut. The former challenges them more to think about providing the current level of service with the less funding. The later just causes them to cut at the margins and not think of doing business differently.

In my experience, this process has generated millions of dollars of savings that has resulted, in many instances, in delivering the same level of services for a reduced cost. It also creates a more positive feeling for the departments when you are able to restore funding rather than to tell them what they need to cut.

One last point on budget reduction strategies is also very important and not often recognized. Since salaries are the biggest cost item, a reduced budget generally means reducing staffing levels. Though many positions in my organizations have been needed to be cut over the years, even up to as many as 500, there never had to be a layoff of employees. In fact, the year we needed to cut 500 positions, we guaranteed that all employees would still have a position with the city. We undertook a very aggressive program to place anyone whose position was to be cut into another position with the city, which was vacant. This necessitated a big effort from human resources and considering all positions across all departments as well as people looking at alternative assignments. This guarantee did a lot to calm the fears of employees and help us all get through difficult times.

Rating agency visits

While not always reflective of the financial well-being of a city or county, the credit rating of a local government is important not only as a reflection of what an outsider's evaluation shows about its credit worthiness but also as a measure of how its finances are managed. The rating is also an important determinant of how much it costs to borrow funds for capital projects. Some local governments put a great deal of emphasis on their rating, and elected officials will use it to show the public that they are doing a good job governing the city or county. When I worked as the County Administrator for Hennepin County, I was very often reminded by the board of commissioners how important the AAA credit rating was and that if the county ever lost the lofty level, I would be out the door.

In theory and mostly in practice, a credit rating reflects the quality of fiscal management, the amount of reserve funds available, the health of the local economy and the willingness of the governing body to set taxes and fees at a level that will support the city's operation. Local governments that score high in all these areas can indeed achieve the highest rating of AAA. However, even the best managed cities with excellent reserves will struggle to achieve an AAA rating if the local economy is not strong. If a city has a lower than average median household income, the rating agencies do not see that city as a good credit risk as would be typical of AAA-rated cities.

While not all factors involved in a credit rating evaluation can be controlled by a city, managers can move the needle on most of them.

Maintaining an adequate reserve fund is critically important. While there is a lot of difference of opinion about what is adequate, most would argue that the reserves should be at least equal to or more than one month's operating revenue. This would be roughly 8.3% of the operating budget. Some may argue it should be at least 3 months operating revenue. My experience tells me that three month's revenue is too much money to hold in reserve when there are always a lot of projects to be funded, which are important to a city's well-being and that level of reserve is not necessary to achieve an AAA rating.

A good example can be the comparison between Greenville County, South Carolina and the City of Greenville. The county has always maintained a very high level of reserves and the city much less. While the city had received a tick below an AAA credit rating, it did achieve the gold standard with still much less reserve than the county. It achieved that through being well managed (sorry for the inherent bias I have here as the former manager), having a strong economy and being willing to invest in improving the city. The county could have maintained its AAA credit rating with much less reserve funds. I am intentionally not describing the level of reserves because one cannot target a specific level and think that will bring an AAA credit rating. So many other factors come into play. In addition, achieving the AAA standard by increasing reserves to a high level is not always in the interest of the locality. The real difference in the cost of borrowing between a city with an AAA rating and one with a slightly lower rate is not that significant. Circumstances may dictate that a city is better off investing some of what would be a higher than necessary level of funds into projects that help its economic well-being and build wealth for its residents. Ultimately, it is a judgment call but one that the manager can make based on what the level of potential investment could bring to the city.

Whether the locality has an AAA rating or a BB rating, a manager should always be thinking about presenting the city in the best light and making the best case for the highest rating possible. Even an upgrade from AA to AA+ can mean a lot in the cost of a bond issue. And managers should not be hesitant to go to New York to meet with the credit rating agencies in their offices. This will greatly increase the likelihood of achieving the best rating you can get. After I became the Newport News City Manager, I noted that the city had not been to visit the credit rating folks for some time. It appeared that this was partially an outgrowth of some controversy surrounding a previous visit in which the city attendees did not show an appropriate level of discretion with their expenses. Nevertheless, my experience told me that going could make a difference in the cost of an impending bond issue.

We put together a very good case for our credit worthiness and traveled with our financial advisors to New York. We pressed the agencies (most tactfully and cheerfully) for an improved rating. We were successful in getting an upgrade to AA+, which not only saved us three million dollars in financing costs but also resulted in a "premium" of seven million dollars. A premium is an amount of money available beyond the bonded level. This enabled us to save money as well as fund a police precinct building. Going to New York made all the difference in our ability to present the city in the best light and actually obtain an increase.

Funding nonprofits

One might imagine that a manager would feel particularly good about their city being able to give assistance to nonprofit community organizations that provide critically needed services or enhance the quality of life in the community. While this can certainly be the case, there is also a significant amount of controversy that can accompany decisions for which organizations to fund and which not to fund as well as how much each gets. I have certainly found this to be the case. This occurs frequently, at least in part, because each of the nonprofits has some form of constituency and those advocates are often very passionate about the organizations they support. Additionally, councils sometimes find these types of decisions easier to understand and relate to than others.

There is certainly a wide range in the nature of the services provided by nonprofit organizations in any community. It will likely range from those providing critical mental health, food security and social services to those serving art, culture and education. Deciding how much to allocate to different kinds of services can be challenging enough, but deciding which different type of organizations to fund can present real challenges. Sorting through all this is helpful when there are different types of funding that may already be earmarked for certain categories of services. For instance, previous council direction may have designated revenue generated from visitors to the city, such as a tax on transient lodging, to be earmarked for activities that generate tourism, such as a hotel and convention bureau or museums, which attract out-of-town visitors. It is also helpful when councils have previously indicated those agencies that they would like to fund. However, councils change and their priorities change. So how can a manager logically approach these funding decisions?

One excellent strategy is to seek community involvement. This is more than just finding someone else to blame for the decisions. Engaging the community allows the values and judgments of a broader cross section of residents to help share in the decision-making. A group formed for some other purpose or formed specifically to develop funding recommendations can be most helpful. I would encourage these to be cast as just recommendations to the manager, not the actual funding decision or recommendations to the council. While a manager certainly would want to follow the committee's recommendations, I was always more comfortable retaining the authority to correct for an obvious bias that the group may have.

It is also most helpful to go through some type of application process that requires certain information from each applicant, which can confirm their nonprofit status as well as their viability as a going concern. The application should also ask for a definitive deliverable that would result if the funding were provided. If the city does provide the funding, then it should be subject to the delivery of that service. It is also helpful to see what funding from other sources might be leveraged by the city funds. I will later cite an incident when this was particularly helpful.

If there is not a source of money that is designated for funding nonprofits or the decision on recommendations of not only what to fund but also how much to allocate for nonprofits is necessary, it is helpful to a have a discussion with the council on priorities prior to making any individual recommendations. Even where there are no firm rules in place, you can always let history help guide the process, modified, of course, by current conditions. For instance, in tight budget years where the funding for staff operations needs to be cut back, cutting back an equal amount from the funding for nonprofits makes sense. Tying the amount of funding to specific accomplishable objectives can be a helpful place to start. For instance, if the city had an objective to increase visitors to the city, there should be a goal established for the amount of the increase the organizations requesting funding would accomplish through their services and how they will contribute to reaching that goal.

I believe that any funding provided to a nonprofit should come with an expected outcome or series of outcomes. This should be included in a contract with the city and the organization should be required to report back to the city on the result at the end of the year.

Nonprofits can often have complicated relationships with the city. I will cite some examples of challenging funding decisions to further explore this topic. When I assumed the position of City Manager for Newport News, Virginia, in 2013, I needed to deal with the sensitive issue of funding the Virginia Living Museum, a combination zoo and aquarium. The museum was built on city land and had been a fixture in the community for almost 50 years. They were experiencing some challenging times financially due to the downturn in the economy in 2008–9 that had not fully recovered, the loss of school system revenue as another outcome of the downturn and a major flood of their facility. There had been a base level of funding of $600,000 that had been provided for many years. However, in the budget I inherited, the city had more than doubled that allocation due to the challenging financial times. There was some push back on that, particularly from one outspoken council member, who preferred them to rely more on private donations and program revenue. Some other council members were supporters of the museum and yet others were more on the fence.

The museum was undertaking a significant private fundraising effort. I saw this as an opportunity to create a win for everyone. I talked to the museum director and chair of their board about the idea of the city funding at the historical level and then using the additional funding that had been provided that year as a challenge grant in the following year. The proposal was that the city would provide a dollar contribution for every two dollars raised by the museum up to the amount of the previous year's extra funding. The reality is that I pretty much knew that the museum could gather sufficient funding to qualify for all the extra funding. However, that was true, in part, because they would be in the position to say to their contributors that this additional match would be available from the city if they contributed. The council unanimously agreed to this approach and the museum did raise enough funds to gain the added funding.

A second example of a city with a complicated relationship with a museum will illustrate some additional difficult issues that can be presented and some approaches to resolving them. When working as a consultant, I led a team brought in to make recommendations to address issues the City of Gastonia was having with its relationship to the Schiele Museum, a science museum operating in the city. This is another situation where the city owned the land and, in this case, the buildings as well. The museum was operated by a museum foundation, a separate operating entity from the city. Some of the employees operating the museum were museum employees and some were city employees. While there had been an attempt to make the compensation and benefit plans similar, there were many important differences. The city provided some funding for the museum operation with the remainder of the funds coming from some program revenues and private donations. In addition, the city retained some of the program revenues.

There were a number of concerns that the city had about the arrangements. The contract that governed the relationship was substantially out of date, and many of the requirements were not being followed. The split in staffing was quite problematic as the staff members were comingled with some city staff reporting to museum staff and vice versa. This had the potential to put the city and the museum at odds with one another if an issue like a harassment complaint arose. Since the benefits were different, there was certainly the possibility of resentment of some employees toward the benefits others received. The financial arrangements were the most troubling to the city as there was a constant struggle each year on how much funding the city would provide. That was also frustrating from the museum's perspective because they did not feel that they could rely on a certain level of funding. Additionally, it was not totally clear which revenue streams went to the city and which went to the museum. The responsibility for maintenance and expansion of the facility was not clearly delineated as well.

So our consulting team was brought in to make recommendations on how to approach the funding level, staffing and capital facility responsibility as well as other contractual issues and recommend a new contract. In addition, we had recommended that we conduct an economic impact assessment for the museum to help demonstrate the value of the museum to the community.

Several important recommendations came out of the study. We felt the split of employees between the city and the museum was quite problematic. We recommended that all employees become city employees. This was driven as much from the employee benefits as anything else. The city employees participated in the state retirement system, a defined benefit plan, whereas the museum employees had a defined contribution plan. The museum employees would not be disadvantaged to move to the city plan, but the city employees would lose the advantage of extra years of service if they were to become museum employees. In order to assist the museum employees who would have had to go through a period to become vested in the city retirement system, we recommended that the city recognize the time they served working for the museum as the time worked for the city.

While the paid leave provisions were similar, the museum employees would lose their accrual rates by becoming new city employees, so we recommended that the museum employment time be credited as if it were time worked for the city.

As we sorted through the financial arrangements, we felt that it would be relatively consistent with the current level of city contribution to set the city funding at an amount that would, along with all the regular museum revenues, cover the basic operations of the museum. Further, that costs for exhibits and enhancements to the operation would be the responsibility of the museum. The museum would pay for these costs through special revenues they raised or private contributions. This provided an incentive for the museum to conduct these programs as well as raise private funds.

While the city would be responsible for the ongoing operations and maintenance of the facilities, the museum would be allowed to compete alongside the city departments for an allocation of capital improvement funds for improvements and the museum would be encouraged to do private fund raising as a match to any city capital funding.

Managing the fiscal affairs of a local government is vitally important for all communities. This is certainly also true for managing the development of our communities. The next chapter explores the issue and solutions for the land use planning and regulation that shapes our communities.

3 Land use planning and regulation

This chapter provides an overall view of the land use patterns and ideal characteristics of communities that would not only address global warming and other environmental objectives but also provide for an efficient use of infrastructure as well as support healthy lifestyle choices. It then moves on to describe more specific planning and regulatory recommendations. It is appropriate to begin with the big picture, an overall perspective of the urbanization of the global population. An online publication produced by Grayline, an advisory and analytics firm entitled, *Urbanization and the Mass Movement of People to Cities*, written by Bret Boyd, describes the scale of the movement to cities in the following way (Boyd n.d.):

> The data is eye-opening. The United Nations in 2009 and the International Organization for Migration in 2015 both estimated that around 3 million people are moving to cities every week. Approximately 54% of people worldwide now live in cities, up from 30% in 1950. Sources estimate this will grow to 2/3 of world population in the next 15-30 years. More than half of urban dwellers live in the 1,022 cities with greater than 500,000 inhabitants. There are currently 29 megacities with populations of over 10 million, up from 2 in 1950 and projected to grow to between 41 and 53 by 2030. Additionally, there are 468 cities with a population of over 1 million, up from 83 in 1950. A Yale research group projects that urban land coverage will expand by 463,000 square miles by 2030 to cover just under 10% of the planet's land, equivalent to 20,000 football fields being paved over every day.

With this movement to cities projected to continue, it is important to consider the best way for cities to grow. The general thrust of the characteristics of this desirable type of development is driven by the

DOI: 10.4324/9781003262756-4

values contained in the Introduction. Preserving the natural environment and reducing the impact that urbanization has on the earth and our nonrenewable resources strongly influence the perspective on the desired nature of development. Additionally, I do not believe that the typical development patterns of US urban areas is the ultimate expression of how human beings would like to live. While people may sometimes express a negative view of higher density development, that does not necessarily mean they would choose a low-density living option. This contradiction was pointed out in an Urban Land Institute study (2005, 2) entitled, *Higher Density Development; Myth and Facts.*.

> Many people's perception of higher-density development does not mesh with the reality. Studies show that when surveyed about higher-density development, those interviewed hold a negative view. But when shown images of higher-density versus lower-density development, people often change their perceptions and prefer higher density. In a recent study by the National Association of Realtors® and Smart Growth America, six in ten prospective homebuyers, when asked to choose between two communities, chose the neighborhood that offered a shorter commute, sidewalks, and amenities like shops, restaurants, libraries, schools, and public transportation within walking distance. They preferred this option over the one with longer commutes and larger lots but limited options for walking. The 2001 American Housing Survey further reveals that respondents cited proximity to work more often than unit type as the leading factor in housing choice. Such contradictions point to widespread misconceptions about the nature of higher-density development and sprawl. Several of these misconceptions are so prevalent as to be considered myths.

I do not believe that low-density development represents the best alternative for urbanized populations to live in harmony with the natural environment. This view is supported in a report from the US Environmental Protection Agency (EPA), entitled, *Protecting Water Resources with Higher-Density Development*, which showed that lower-density development had a larger impact on a watershed than higher densities of development (US EPA 2006, 1).

Beyond the environmental implications, the effectiveness and efficiency of providing infrastructure to serve residential development favors a denser pattern than provided by single family residential development. It is more costly to provide water, wastewater and transportation facilities to single family residential development than to denser residential development and mixed use development as well.

The Real Estate Research (1974) Institute published a three-volume issue on urban sprawl and exploration entitled, *The Costs of Sprawl*, which became the seminal work on the negative effects of urban sprawl. Many studies have followed up on this research. In one such study, the cost to serve different densities of development was documented by the Halifax Regional Municipality in Nova Scotia, Canada. This study of April 2005 entitled, *Healthy Growth for HRM; Settlement Pattern and Form with Service Cost Analysis*, examined the cost of both capital and operating costs to serve developments with varying densities. They examined nine city services: roads, transit, water, wastewater, solid waste, parks and recreation, libraries, police and fire. They found that the cost to serve varies greatly with the density of development with the cost per household for low-density development being many times the cost for the highest density pattern (Halifax Regional Municipality 2005).

It showed a cost of over $5,000 per household for the lowest residential density and less than $1,500 for the highest residential density. I would like to note that as the density increased beyond 36 people per acre, the rate of increase in infrastructure cost was much less. I will reference this later when showing a particular housing development in the Seattle area. If one looks at the average persons per household in Halifax, which is roughly 2.15 persons, the density of housing units at 36 persons per acre becomes a bit more than 16.5 houses per acre.

There have been numerous studies that have examined the cost of development at various densities, and while the costs certainly vary from study to study, the inevitable conclusion is that the cost to service residential development is higher for the lowest residential densities.

Anyone who has flown over both Europe and the United States has observed a remarkable difference in the development patterns. An aerial view over most European areas will show concentrated land uses with large areas of open space either in farm production or in a natural state. While a significant portion of the United States also has large areas of agricultural lands and natural areas, our cities are generally much less concentrated and are, generally, more sprawling. Figure 3.1 shows an aerial view over a French city.

Of course, much of this difference in land use patterns can be attributed to when the development took place. Most European cities began their development centuries ago before the advent of the automobile, which now has a dominate influence on the way cities develop. Many European cities that began to develop centuries ago have subsequently spread much more than the original settlements.

Figure 3.1 An aerial view from Google Earth over a French city.

If one takes a closer look at the development patterns, one finds a higher level of mixing of land uses in the older European cities and much more separation of land uses in their US counterparts. A large number of urban planners in the United States have recognized that the nature of our development was either enabled or driven, depending on your perspective, by the automobile, consumes large amounts of land and wastes a tremendous amount of energy. The separation of land uses and sprawling residential development necessitates long commute to work times and leads to lost productivity. Many also feel that these patterns lead to social isolation. Figures 3.2 and 3.3 show examples of sprawl development in US cities.

In addition, the low-density suburban development that has characterized a large portion of the development in this country has greatly contributed to greenhouse gas (GHG) emissions. Authors of a report from the Brookings Institute describe the situation, as follows (Tomer, Kane, Schuetz and George 2021):

> Simply put, the United States cannot reach its GHG reduction targets if our urban areas continue to grow as they have in the past. After decades of sprawl, the U.S. has the dubious honor of

Figure 3.2 An aerial photograph from Google Earth showing sprawled development in the Los Angeles area.

Figure 3.3 A three-dimensional aerial view from Google showing sprawled development in the Los Angeles area.

being a world leader in both building-related energy consumption and vehicle miles traveled per capita. Making matters worse, lower-density development also pollutes our water and requires higher relative emissions during the initial construction.

In the same article, the authors compare two neighborhoods in Kansas City with approximately the same number of residents. In an older neighborhood that was built prior to automobile dominance and based more on walking and transit, the neighborhood took up 0.3 of a square mile. A newer neighborhood, built around the automobile, consumed 1.4 square miles. When the authors looked at the change in the amount of urbanized area in the United States, they found that that area increased at a rate 1.7 times greater than the rate of increase in the population.

In addition to the environmental benefits of a more concentrated land use pattern, I believe that people are, by nature, social animals and enjoy a relatively high level of interaction with one another. More concentrated and mixed land uses facilitate the opportunity for this level of interaction. The significant trend for many people to move back to the denser areas of cities is reflective of this desire for interaction. A great example of this is the City of Seattle, Washington. I worked for the city back in the 1980s. When I left the city in 1987, the population of the city was less than 500,000. Without any expansion of its boundaries, the city's population now exceeds 750,000. Along with this, population has been an explosion of the high-tech employment in the city. More and more tech firms are growing in the city because the workers want to be there.

While Seattle may be a special case, central city areas all over the country have seen growth of residents who want to live in a more concentrated pattern and closer to their places of employment. People have been willing to pay a premium to live closer to work and other activities. Of course, this is more prevalent among singles and couples without children. Families with children tend to put more value on a less dense environment and live more often outside of the central area of cities.

This has often meant that families have frequently settled in a sub-urban single family detached from home. I would argue that the movement to a suburban lifestyle has been driven by a romanticized notion of an ideal environment to live in and raise a family as well as the notion that this represents a successful attainment of status. Indeed, the bigger and more elaborate the house, the more status that the family has attained. Larger lots have been perceived as more impressive than smaller ones. The ubiquitous use of automobiles allows for transportation to a relatively low-density suburban setting. Along with the lower-density single family development comes the extensive consumption of land and the spread of development. This has also resulted in long commutes to places of work. In order for some to be able to afford this single family relatively low-density environment, they have had to locate further and further away from centers of employment. In the Los Angeles metropolitan area, it has resulted in some commuting two hours or more in each direction. This suburban idealized notion of success and what is best for a family environment has also driven the choices of people by focusing what types of housing are on the market and available to people.

However, is this truly an ideal environment for families and is it the best for the environment? Are there alternatives that satisfy the needs of people and are better for the environment? What characteristics would be important in an alternative environment? I suggest that the following aspects are important for families:

- Connection to the ground
- Readily available, close by open space
- A measure of privacy
- Access to transportation work, school, shopping and entertainment trips
- Proximity to other families with children
- Home ownership

While one can raise a family in a high-density, high-rise building environment, I think that most people would argue that this is not ideal. However, environments characterized by townhomes and readily available open space can represent an excellent environment for families. The community I currently live, 12 Degrees North, can serve as a very good example. It is a development of 27 single family homes and 86 townhouses. There is substantial open space that, for most of the townhouses, is outside their front door. Everyone has an attached garage for ready access to their automobile. Yet the development has a density of 16 units per acre and consumes a lot less land than even medium to higher-density single family homes. Additionally, it does still provide the option for some to choose a detached home. It is also close to a bus line with great access to the central city. While there are many singles and couples without children living in the development, there are also lots of families raising children. While homeownership is not a physical aspect of a development, it can be valuable for wealth building for the family. Figure 3.4 is a picture of the 12 Degrees North community.

Figure 3.4 A picture of the 12 Degrees North community photographed by
the author.

It is very difficult to serve a low-density single family area with transit
service, and therefore, the residents need to rely on automobiles, which
presents its own challenges for the environment. Some ability for transit
to be among the transportation options can have a huge benefit for the
environment.

For those of you who are uptight about this discussion and the
implications for single family neighborhoods, I am not advocating their
elimination. Rather, I am suggesting that we can consider alternatives
that would have many benefits. This will be the lens through which this
chapter views much of the land use planning and regulatory controls
recommendations.

Managing growth

The idea of managing growth in a community is often as volatile an
issue as any that managers will experience in cities and counties across
the country. I certainly experienced this in many places, particularly
in Hillsborough County, Florida, when serving as a senior county

administrator responsible for land use planning and regulation as well as infrastructure, among other functions. Growth issues have been paramount in local government politics for decades in Florida. This has resulted in council majorities fluctuating from pro-growth to growth control and back again, which has led to significant instability. In fact, it is my opinion that this is a major contributor to the high turnover of managers in Florida communities. The new majorities on councils do not believe that the incumbent manager will follow the policies they would like to change. They associate the policies of the previous council with the manager and fail to grasp the concept that it is the council setting the policies, not the manager. Of course, there are other reasons for new council majorities changing managers, including just wanting to appoint "their own person."

The idea of "managing growth" means a lot of different things to different people. To some it is a request for the last person in to shut the door and the desire to stop virtually all growth. To others it may reflect a desire to prevent an increase in the density of development. Yet others may want to stop increases in traffic or at least control the increases. It can also mean achieving a more compact development pattern or preserving open space or even accommodating growth through an aggressive program of providing public infrastructure to support growth.

For the purpose of this discussion, I will define managing growth as controlling the type of development and its location and ensuring that there are public facilities in place that are capable of accommodating the development.

Taking into consideration the values outlined in the introduction and the concerns that people generally express about new development, I recommend that policies to manage growth should focus on the following objectives:

- Ensure that adequate public infrastructure is in place at the time of the development to accommodate the impacts of the development.
- Develop a plan to preserve sufficient open space and ensure that it will be preserved.
- Permit development that will result in a compact land use pattern that can be effectively and efficiently served by transit and other infrastructure.
- Promote a mixture of land uses that encourage walking trips and reduce the need for automobile travel.
- Allow for a variety of housing types with a minimal number of single family detached homes.

- Encourage a balance in home ownership and rental options to meet the community's needs.

Adequate public facilities

In 1985, the State of Florida developed what, at the time, was the most progressive growth management legislation in the nation. Arguably the linchpin of this law was the requirement dubbed, *concurrency*. This concurrency provision required that public facilities that are adequate to serve a development must be in place at the time of the impact of the land uses. It further restricted cities or counties from issuing a certificate of occupancy to any development prior to the completion of the necessary public facilities. These facilities included transportation, water, wastewater, stormwater and parks and recreation. One of my responsibilities when I was appointed in 1987 as an Assistant County Administrator with Hillsborough County was to lead the county's development of regulations to meet this concurrency requirement.

In formulating the regulations to meet concurrency, each community was required to set a level of service standard for each type of public facility and ensure that any new development did not cause this level of service standard to be exceeded. If the level of service would be exceeded, the developer could choose to build or expand facilities sufficient to accommodate the impact of their development. This could mean building or expanding a roadway or assisting the city with traffic signal improvements that would be sufficient to accommodate the development's impacts. Similar types of improvements could be made to other facilities such as expanding water or wastewater pipes or treatment facilities to accommodate the development.

Examining the type of standards generally set for the transportation system will provide a good example. Most managers have some familiarity with the system of levels of service for roads, which are classified with letters ranging from A through F. A is the best level of service and is characterized by a free flow of traffic. B also has a free flow of traffic, but there is a growing degree of interactions of vehicles. Level C is where there is substantial flow and more interactions among vehicles but the general speeds at which vehicles travel is not degraded. At level of service D, there is a substantial reduction in speed, and vehicles may have to wait through more than one cycle of a light to clear the intersection. Level E is characterized by a further reduced speed and frequently not making it through traffic lights without waiting at least one extra cycle. The final level, F, is when the traffic flow totally breaks down and gridlock can occur where traffic does not necessarily clear an intersection and the traffic coming from the other intersecting street cannot proceed. The level of service that has been set as a standard is generally either C or D. A level of service C has been more often used in a less developed community, and those substantially urbanized places have more often adopted a level of service D.

While implementing the concurrency requirement has some complexity, I think it is the best approach to reducing the negative aspects of development for a community. The State of Washington has also instituted a requirement for adequate public facilities and implemented a concurrency provision. However, it is only mandated for transportation and is optional for other types of facilities. Maryland state law mandates a public facilities plan as part of the locality's comprehensive plan, and it must include a funding plan to pay for facilities that are necessary. It also allows for the adoption of an adequate public facilities ordinance.

Even though some states have taken a similar approach, it has not gained a broad acceptance. Other approaches result in some similar types of outcomes. For instance, communities that require traffic studies to be made as part of the approval process often require that a development should not reduce the level of service on a roadway. However, in many instances, the requirement is just that the roadway condition not get any worse than at the time of the proposal. Of course, this does not address the problem of an already inadequate facility. While there are different approaches, the straightforward requirement for adequate public facilities offers an excellent method to deal with these impacts. This is particularly appropriate for handling transportation facilities and should include transit as well. While it is also a good approach for water and wastewater, it is not as critical because state laws generally do not allow municipalities to issue permits for development unless adequate capacity exists to supply water or collect and treat wastewater. Localities also are generally not allowed to issue permits without adequate provision for stormwater drainage. It is harder to establish a direct correlation to parks and recreation and schools. However, there is a possibility to charge impact fees for those facilities.

Impact/capacity fees

Just as in Chapter 2, I will advocate for the appropriate use of impact or capacity fees. Capacity fees for water and wastewater are well established and are an essential tool to stay up with the needs of new development. The fees do need to be calculated to be the true additional cost to the system to pay for needed capacity. Transportation fees are also an excellent solution to add funding for system improvement and need to be tailored to the cost of meeting the additional demand.

While impact fees for parks and recreation are an option, consideration must be given to the amount charged for development fees and maintaining a competitiveness with other surrounding jurisdictions. I think a better approach is to plan for open space and encourage developers to cluster development and leave significant open space as part of the community. This brings the land in close proximity to the residents of an area.

School impact fees can also be considered. However, establishing a rational nexus between the fee and the amount charged for development is more problematic. It would not be appropriate to charge for anything but residential development and that is a tenuous rational nexus for many residential projects. Given the challenges with impact fees for schools, I think that it is better to pursue other funding options.

Phased infrastructure expansion

While ensuring that adequate public infrastructure is available for development and the funding of those facilities is important, it is also critical to have a planned, phased expansion of the services to support development. Simply providing water, wastewater, transportation and other facilities wherever and whenever someone wants to develop would result in an uneconomical and poorly planned community. Cities and counties should plan to extend services from adjacent development outward as the pace of needed development warrants it.

This does not imply that local governments can restrict all development to the area where utilities are planned. In cases where the state has aggressive growth boundary legislation such as Oregon, communities can be more aggressive in restricting the expansion of the developed area. However, courts in other states have required jurisdictions to allow development in areas not planned for growth if the developer will pay for extending the services. On the other hand, this may not be practically feasible and more contiguous development can still be achieved.

Land use planning/zoning

Appropriate planning for the development of land uses and the controls put in place to implement those plans are essential. This is certainly not going to be a thorough discussion of land use planning and zoning but rather an exploration of the principles that are often not followed but are critically important as well as an examination of some considerations for managers. The most critical advice for managers is to be engaged in the planning and land use control process. While it is critical to employ outstanding planning professionals and to rely on their expertise and judgment, managers cannot afford to be just innocent bystanders. There is too much at stake.

One of the best examples I can relate is when I assumed the position as the Newport News City Manager. The very first meeting of the City Council involved a major land use decision that would have long-term repercussions on the economic well-being of the city and its inhabitants for years to come. This decision was whether to grant a rezoning to accommodate a large retail component of a massive mixed-use project that would ultimately provide for thousands of jobs, economic stimulus and an enhanced quality of life. In addition to the shopping center, the development would include residential space, a health club and approximately one million square feet of office/research space. Approval of the retail development was essential for the entire development to proceed.

Approval of this project was far from a slam dunk even though it had been billed as a critically important project during the city manager recruitment process I had just finished going through. I needed to assess whether this was truly in the city's interest and whether it fit within the priorities and policies of the city council. There was no question that this not only fit with the overall desires of the council but also was clearly in the short- and long-term public interest. It was also supported by the planning and economic development professionals, and all public facility impacts were handled appropriately.

Even though there was a support of staff, and it was such a critical project, there was a significant chance it would not be approved due to opposition of many in an adjacent development. In addition, while this was in a built-up area, much of the large track of land had been left in an undeveloped state. I felt that it was essential to become engaged and advocate for the project. Whether or not that ultimately made the difference, the lack of the city manager's support could have been very problematic. There are times when the manager must be very involved in land use decisions for the good of the community. Since there was only one council meeting in August when this was being heard and I started in mid-July when there were no council meetings, I had some time to be able to provide support for the proposal. This retail project as well as the residential and office/research buildings that have followed are on their way to making a major difference in the vitality of the city.

Just as there are times when a manager needs to be engaged in land use control administration, it is also quite true in the development of a comprehensive plan. There are books written about comprehensive planning to guide planners and their supervisors. However, there are several aspects of the comprehensive planning process that are critical for city managers and local government leaders to be engaged with. Long-range plans are vehicles to implement the vision and policies of the city council and need the oversight of the manager. The entire planning program of a community needs to be driven by the comprehensive plan, sometimes referred to as the general plan. Unfortunately, some communities reduce the plan to not much more than a glorified zoning plan. When serving as the Community Development Director for Cherry Hill, New Jersey, my responsibilities included the planning and land use functions for the city. In many New Jersey communities, the "comprehensive plan" is done on a base map, which includes property boundaries. That is no way to do a policy document to guide the long-term future of a community. Such a plan needs to provide overall guidance and a framework for individual land use decisions that are affected by the conditions existing at the time of the proposed development. Those conditions and their circumstances can hardly be fully anticipated when a comprehensive plan is adopted.

Additionally, comprehensive plans need to include public facility plans, especially transportation, that are closely tied to the land use element. It is critical that the capacities of the planned public facilities are sufficient to serve the projected land use development that could be accommodated. It is amazing how often this linkage is not sufficient.

Land use decisions can certainly become political, and while I think there are times when a manager should become involved, he or she needs to be cognizant of the council dynamics and the real potential of getting caught in the middle. Another example from my time as the Newport News City Manager can vividly illustrate this. Newport News is home to the Newport News/Williamsburg International Airport. In my previous book, I go into a situation related to the airport that became very difficult for me personally but will not repeat the story for those who have read it and just leave it as a tease to encourage those who have not read it to do so. As way of background, I was appointed by the city council to serve on the airport authority board of directors. Thus, I was wearing two hats when a developer proposed to buy a piece of airport property and develop a retail facility. The airport would have benefited substantially from enhanced revenue from the development, and the city's financial gain would have been extensive as well. I checked with both the airport board attorney and the city attorney to confirm that neither felt I had any conflict of interest in this issue. Since it was in the interest of both parties that this development go forward and I had no personal financial interest, both the attorneys agreed that there was no conflict of interest. This was also because while I was in a decision-making capacity for the airport, I was not for the city.

The principal tenant in the retail proposal was to be a Wegmans grocery and mixed retail store. For those readers not familiar with Wegmans, they are an upscale chain based in New York State that has been expanding along the east coast. The stores are generally very large; the one proposed for Newport News was 140,000 square feet and included restaurants and other nongrocery items for sale. The revenue to the city for this project would have exceeded one million dollars annually.

The site was close to an interstate interchange tying I-64 with the most heavily traveled arterial in the city. It was obvious why this was a very attractive site for Wegmans, which would draw from the entire region. If the project had been proposed a year earlier, it would have had a much greater chance of success. However, the land use action, which involved a comprehensive plan change as well as a zoning amendment, was just prior to a city council election.

While there were other relatively less important concerns raised by an adjacent neighborhood, traffic was the principal issue residents complained about. Indeed, the existing traffic conditions did include a significant amount of congestion with the interstate exit ramp entering the arterial just before the site. However, the developer and their traffic engineer had come up with an excellent plan of improvements, which would not only handle the added traffic but also greatly improve the traffic flow over the existing conditions. This would clearly be a win-win for everyone.

As one could imagine, many of the residents did not see it as a win and distrusted the developer and city professionals. Some of this was frankly an outgrowth of the level of distrust of government officials that exists in the country today. It was also an outgrowth of a meeting the developer had with the residents in the area that did not go well. The resident's opposition was stoked by a city council member who was running for reelection who felt that she could gain votes by rallying the neighbors against the project and, thus, be their champion. This then put other council members running for their seats in a difficult position.

Despite the great advantages of the project, the City of Newport News became the first place in the country to reject a Wegmans. Not a wonderful claim to fame. If there is a moral to the story, the old adage that timing is everything applies. Despite my previous urging of the developers to proceed sooner, their delay cost them the project. With the delay, they would have been better served by waiting until after the election.

Land use permitting

The final issue for this chapter is the land use permitting approval process itself. This process can be very disjointed, inefficient and ineffective when multiple city departments are engaged in the review process, especially when they are located in a variety of places. This was certainly true when I assumed my position with Hillsborough County. Developers were frustrated with the time the process took, the sometimes conflicting requirements from different departments and the multiple review of plans that were often required before an approval was granted. On the other hand, the county staff was frustrated with poor quality of submittals, their comments being countermanded by staff from other departments and their lack of awareness of where a project was in the process.

In order to address this situation, we instituted a one-stop permitting operation that included the colocation of at least one staff representative from each department involved in the review process. In addition, there was one manager assigned to be responsible for the center's operation. Developers had one point of contact and could meet with a departmental representative for any concern the county would have. This resulted in a coordinated response and fewer conflicts among the departments.

There are many instances where a consolidated permitting center will make sense. Additionally, there are now automated permitting systems that are a great benefit for the development review process and should be used by any locality with multiple departments involved in reviewing plans. They also provide the benefit of giving the developer a real-time view of the status of their project. Also, using an electronic plan submission and review process is the state of the art for communities.

Closely related to the land use and planning concerns are the critically important environmental issues we face. The next chapter provides a perspective on the need to be better stewards of our environment.

References

Boyd, Bret. n.d. "Urbanization and the Mass Movement of People to Cities." Accessed August 19, 2021. *Grayline*. https://graylinegroup.com/urbanization-catalyst-overview/.

Halifax Regional Municipality. 2005. *Healthy Growth for HRM; Settlement Pattern and Form with Service Cost Analysis*. Halifax: Halifax Regional Municipality.

Real Estate Research Institute. 1974. *The Cost of Sprawl*. Washington, DC: US Government Printing Office.

Tomer, Adie, Kane, Joseph W., Schuetz, Jenny and George, Caroline. 2021. "We Can't Beat the Climate Crisis without Rethinking Land Use". Accessed August 20, 2021. *Brookings Institute.* www.brookings.edu/research/we-cant-beat-the-climate-crisis-without-rethinking-land-use/

Urban Land Institute. 2005. "Higher Density Development; Myth and Fact". Accessed August 19, 2021. https://uli.org/wp-content/uploads/ULI Documents/HigherDensity_MythFact.ashx_.pdf.

US EPA. 2006. *Protecting Water Resources with Higher-Density Development.* Washington, DC: US EPA, 1.

4 Environmental stewardship

It is hard to believe that anyone would challenge the idea that global warming is real and represents a grave threat to our planet and life as we know it on earth. According to the National Oceanic and Atmospheric Administration (NOAA), 2016 was the warmest year on record and 2020 was only slightly behind it (National Oceanic and Atmospheric Administration 2021). In the same report, NOAA says that the earth is almost two degrees warmer than it was before the turn of the century. Death Valley recorded a temperature of 129.9 degrees, the hottest temperature ever recorded. Phoenix saw over 144 days over 100 degrees and 53 days over 110 degrees. The 53 days over 110 degrees was 20 days more than the previous record of 33 days. And I thought that it was hot in the Phoenix area when I lived there from 1997 to 2004! The glacial ice is melting near the north and south poles at alarming rates. The hurricane season has seen one record-setting storm after another, with more named storms in 2020 than any previous year (Scientific American 2020). While this does not fit the narrative of those who would deny the problem so that they can trump other issues at the expense of environmental protection, the truth of global warming is undeniable. While local government managers cannot make the same statements as a retired manager like me, they still have an affirmative obligation to help the earth survive. We all have a critical stake in creating a sustainable future.

The effects of global warming are evident today, and the future effects are daunting at best. Coastal cities are threatened by sea level rise. Rising temperatures are a great health risk, especially to seniors who do not have air conditioning. Droughts are putting large parts of the country at risk. The danger of massive, uncontrollable fires is readily evident from recent years. In 2020, California had the five of the six largest fires in their history with over four million acres burned, which was

DOI: 10.4324/9781003262756-5

double the previous record (Anguiano 2020). Also in 2020, Colorado experienced the three largest fires in the state's history.

Although there are a great many wonderful books written, I do not generally give many recommendations. However, there is one book that ought to be a required reading for everyone. *Cradle to Cradle: Remaking the Way We Make Things* by William McDonough and Michael Braungart (Braungart and McDonough 2002) provides a perspective on the production and reuse of materials and goods that could transform the amount of waste we produce. The central theme of the book is to view the production things and the use of materials throughout the entire life cycle of materials. When something is produced, we need to make it in a way that it can be reused and/or the materials recycled. Furthermore, we need to only make things in ways that will not harm the environment. For instance, why would we make the plastic products that hold cans of soda together when they cannot biodegrade and will end up strangling the fish in the ocean when there are other easy ways to replace this product.

Granted, changing the rules governing production might be made at a level of government beyond cities and counties, but all products *are* made in a city or a county or both and those governments are not without influence. If the manufacturer were responsible for the reuse of what they produce, the products they make would be very different from what it is today. We would create a more sustainable world.

Sustainability is certainly a trendy word today. Wikipedia says that "Sustainability is the ability to exist constantly. In the 21st century, it refers generally to the capacity for the biosphere and human civilization to co-exist." (Wikipedia, n.d.)

City/county actions to reduce global warming

It is crystal clear that global warming presents a crisis for the plant and we must act. The actions to develop a more efficient land use pattern have been discussed in an earlier chapter. Governments must act and local governments can make a huge difference. Cities and counties need to take actions that promote carbon neutrality, both in their operations and for all activities within the boundaries as well. Being carbon neutral means to not increase carbon dioxide emissions through any activity such as making a product or transporting something either by reducing emissions to offset any increase or not producing any with the activity. By reducing carbon dioxide, we will reduce the largest cause of global warming.

The concept of *carbon credits* was introduced to encourage reducing greenhouse gases. A carbon credit is a commodity that can be traded to give an offset for the equivalent giving off one ton of carbon dioxide. The market value for these credits varies greatly by location. As of February 2021, the market value for a carbon credit in Europe was slightly less than $50 per ton of carbon dioxide equivalent according to a report produced by *The Economist* (2021). Europe has the overwhelming amount of carbon credit trading. The price in the United States is a small fraction of this but is expected to grow based on the goals for GHG reductions set by the Biden Administration.

The reader may be asking themselves what does the price of carbon credits have to do with city and county management. There are potential instances in which local governments could generate carbon credits that would be marketable to private businesses in their efforts to achieve carbon emissions neutrality. For instance, this could be used as a funding source for certain projects when a private company would come in to do a project that would result in carbon credits that they could then sell on the open market.

There are some definitive strategies that cities and counties can pursue to help counteract global warming, including the following:

- Taking steps to reduce or at least slow the increase in automobile travel by enhancing public transportation options, promoting mixed use development and more concentrated land use patterns.
- Preserving the natural environment and expanding green space throughout the community.
- Encouraging alternate fuel automobiles through providing charging stations and transitioning their fleet to nongas vehicles.
- Promoting the development and use of renewable energy sources such as solar and wind power.
- Conserving energy by retrofitting existing buildings and requiring energy efficiencies in new structures.
- Banning plastic bag use.
- Better managing the waste stream including enhanced recycling and use of composting.
- Planting trees and other vegetation.
- Adopting other strategies to reduce air quality pollutants.
- Adopting practices when holding events that minimize the negative environmental effects.

While some of the strategies to address the land use issues are described in the proceeding chapter, the later chapters on transportation and public facilities will describe some of the strategies to address some of the previous points. The following is a discussion on some of the additional points.

Air quality

Improving air quality will not only assist in reducing global warming but will also have significant health benefits for residents. The US Environmental Protection Agency regulates six different air quality pollutants: carbon monoxide, ground-level ozone, lead, nitrogen oxides, particulate matter and sulfur dioxide. While I served as the Executive Director of the Phoenix regional planning organization, the organization was responsible for the air quality planning. The region was classified as a nonattainment area for carbon monoxide, ozone and particulates. That is, we exceeded the required maximum of each pollutant. We operated very sophisticated urban airshed models to replicate the atmospheric conditions and the amount of existing pollution of each of these issues. We developed plans to decrease the levels of each of these pollutants and show the results using these models. In this way, we hoped to be able to show how we would be able to be in "attainment." During the course of my tenure, we were able to bring the region into an attainment status for each air quality issue.

While a large number of managers are not familiar with regional air quality issues, it can present a major issue for communities and managers need to be informed about the regulations and issues they involve. Regions that are classified as not being in attainment or do not have an approved plan to get to attainment are not allowed to go forward with building their transportation improvements. In a later chapter, I will describe a situation that almost put a halt to the Phoenix area projects and did cause a suspension of projects in many large urban areas of the county.

Natural area preservation

Preserving the natural environment or restoring land into a more natural state not only improves air quality but also greatly enhances the quality of life in a community. Residents are placing increasing value on open space and, in particular, trees and vegetation. This can be achieved through excellent land use planning and control practices as well as land purchases and dedications. Clustering development and preserving open space will pay great dividends for years and balance the economics of development projects with the quality of life of a community. In many communities, bond issues for open space preservation have met with voter approval. Additionally, the use of property tax reductions for open space conservation easements has been very successful. For example, in 2020, voters approved all 26 measures for land conservation, parks, climate resiliency and habitat in 11 different states. This included a $3.7 billion measure in the State of California.

While the environment is certainly a pressing concern, this is certainly true for the housing in our communities. That is taken up in the following chapter.

References

Anguiano, Danny. 2020. "California Wildfire Hell: How 2020 Became the State's Worst Ever Fire Season". *The Guardian*. December 30, 2020.

Braungart, Michael and McDonough, William. 2002. *Cradle to Cradle: Remaking the Way We Make Things*. New York: North Point Press.

National Oceanic and Atmospheric Administration. 2021. "Global Climate Report-Annual 2020". Accessed August 20, 2021. www.ncdc.noaa.gov/sotc/global/202013

Scientific American. 2020. "A Running List of Record-Breaking Natural Disasters in 2020". Accessed August 20, 2021. www.scientificamerican.com/article/a-running-list-of-record-breaking-natural-disasters-in-2020/

The Economist. 2021. "Prices in the World's Biggest Carbon Market Are Soaring". February 27, 2021. www.economist.com/finance-and-economics/2021/02/24/prices-in-the-worlds-biggest-carbon-market-are-soaring

Wikipedia. 2021. "Sustainability". Accessed August 20, 2021. https://en.wikipedia.org/wiki/Sustainability

5   Housing

Chapter 3 included recommendations for the type of housing that is best suited for a large portion of urbanized areas. This chapter delves into the difficult issues of providing for affordable housing, the dilemma of gentrification and the challenge of homelessness. These three issues have concerned local governments for decades. While many have sought answers to these matters, definitive answers have been difficult to come by for most communities. This chapter will not include a full discussion of all the facets of these concerns but rather will present approaches that can help resolve the problems that communities face.

Affordable housing

The term *affordable housing* has been used in a wide variety of ways and certainly means something different in various locations and with various groups. For the purpose of this discussion, affordable housing refers to housing that costs no more than 30% of the resident's income including rent or mortgage payment, property taxes and fees as well as utilities for incomes that are no more than 60% of the median family income for the area in which they are located. While the 30% amount is generally the standard percentage of income, the amount of income does vary from program to program. However, 60% is currently the most often used standard by the Department of Housing and Urban Development (HUD).

Affordable housing is also frequently referred to as *low- and moderate-income housing*. This term will be used in a similar fashion as affordable housing in the foregoing discussion.

Many cities do look at housing affordability for higher wage earners as well. This is often the concern in higher cost jurisdictions where those employed as police officers, firemen or teachers may make more

DOI: 10.4324/9781003262756-6

than 60% of the median household income yet still cannot afford to live virtually anywhere in the city where they work. This is often referred to as *working-class housing*. This chapter will focus on some key recommendations that could assist in providing housing for both of these groups.

While there are a great multitude of programs and recommendations to address affordable housing, this focuses on two principle strategies that can make the biggest difference in providing affordable housing. These recommendations are at least partially driven by some critical assumptions based on the long history in this country with providing housing to groups that cannot obtain housing through the free market conditions. I think most experts will agree that the high-rise public housing projects built in this country were a terrible solution for those who lived there. I experienced one of the most infamous examples of this failure when I was in graduate school in St. Louis in the mid-1970s. This public housing project, Pruit-Igoe, when completed in 1956, consisted of 33 buildings 11 stories in height. It quickly became the poster child for crime and poverty and stigmatized those who lived there. It was not only the high-rise configuration that was so ill-suited to its residents but also the tremendous concentration of those with little opportunity to be successful in the local economy. During the time I was in St. Louis, the entire 33 buildings were destroyed.

Among the approaches that I believe should be followed in providing housing include using low-rise housing types where people have a relationship with the ground and avoiding a concentration of affordable housing. The scale of a high-rise building can be overwhelming, making it difficult to develop a sense of community and relationships with neighbors. It also reduces their sense of identification with *their* home, the place where they live and feel good about it. There should be some outside space that is readily available to residents that is not just a large open area shared by hundreds or even thousands of people. Concentrating a lot of affordable housing makes it clear that it is for those who cannot afford market rate housing and promotes a stereotyping of its residents.

Avoiding a concentration in affordable housing goes beyond just building smaller projects but also needs to include spreading them throughout the community. This not only helps break down the stigmatization but also helps reduce segregation. It has often been the case that minorities more often reside in low- and moderate-income housing options. Not only is it desirable to spread housing throughout a community, I argue that it is best to also include affordable housing options in most/all developments.

While the governments have built public housing in the past, this approach has been largely abandoned, in favor of the currently, most accepted model to provide some form of subsidy for private-sector projects with controlled rents or purchase prices.

In addition to outlining the above principles, it is important to discuss the idea of a community's *fair share* of affordable housing. This concept has often been driven by the perceived obligation to include housing in a city that is affordable to those who work in the city. Thus, not only policemen, firemen and teachers but also waiters and janitors could afford housing. It is also driven by the objection that some have to exclusive cities, which, due to either land values or land use controls or a combination of the two, effectively have little or no affordable housing. Perhaps nowhere has the requirement for cities to have their fair share of affordable housing been more institutionalized than in the State of New Jersey. This is due to the court decisions well known to urban planners involving the town of Mount Laurel. Since Cherry Hill is next door to Mount Laurel, I was very involved in this issue when working there.

The two Mount Laurel court decisions ruled that it is the affirmative obligation of every municipality to provide for their fair share of affordable housing and they must have a plan that would include a reasonable expectation that their fair share would be developed. I will not delve into the approaches for calculating fair share as they can vary significantly from place to place. I present this situation because it gave rise to the extensive use of inclusionary zoning approaches.

With these concepts in mind, I offer the following recommendations for achieving affordable housing for communities.

It is important to establish an independent nonprofit housing fund to collect public and private contributions to fund grants, which leverage affordable housing.

- Work to establish nonprofit community development corporations, which could develop housing.
- Devote revenue from the city or county each year to the housing fund.
- Support the use of tax credit programs for developers to build affordable housing.
- Adopt an inclusionary zoning ordinance, which requires a mandatory set aside for affordable housing as part of housing developments and provides for an incentive for including additional affordable housing units through a density bonus.

If a nonprofit housing fund does not exist, the city or county should take the initiative and establish such an entity. While the local government can have representatives on the board that controls the fund, it must be a separate entity to maintain its nonprofit status. The board should have a broad representation from the community, and its members should have the ability to successfully gain contributions to the fund. This entity should provide grants to local developers to assist in the production of affordable housing by providing an increment of additional funding that might make a project work or result in a further write down of the housing price or leverage additional affordable housing units.

The local government should work with existing nonprofit community development corporations where they exist and assist in their development where there is insufficient capacity. These organizations will be able to obtain funding and operate as developers of affordable housing.

It is important that the local government should commit some of its resources to help raise money for the housing fund. There should be a commitment from the council for multiyear funding to provide some measure of certainty for expected funds. While councils generally cannot commit future councils to spending, most subsequent councils generally will go along with such commitments. As an added incentive for public funding, it can be tied to a certain level of private contributions.

State tax credits, which are available for developers producing affordable housing, are a significant source of funding for low- and moderate-income housing and should be encouraged by the city or county. These are often very competitive programs, and the local government's endorsement can be vital. The city or county can also encourage certain priority areas or types of projects.

Inclusionary zoning ordinances can be a terrific vehicle to get affordable housing built in local areas. However, they can often be very controversial and are even prohibited in certain states such as Tennessee. They also come with some implementation challenges. Inclusionary zoning ordinances generally require that housing developments provide a certain percentage of the homes in a development, typically 10%, as affordable housing units. This would include rental or home ownership projects. For rental properties, the rents would be restricted to a certain level, such as rent affordable to 60% of the median family income assuming a 30% expenditure for housing costs. Ownership units would be similarly restricted to a purchase cost affordable for a similar family income. Additionally, the resale of the affordable housing units is generally restricted to the purchase price plus some inflationary adjustment to ensure that the housing will remain affordable. Those who rent or purchase the unit would be screened to ensure that they also meet the income requirements. These restrictive provisions are most often included in the property's deed restrictions.

One of the challenges of inclusionary zoning ordinances is that it may be very difficult for some projects to provide affordable homes due to circumstances such as the size of the project. If there is a 10% requirement, what do you do if there are only four or five units? This could be handled by a fee in lieu requirement. This fee could then be used to help build affordable housing. This, of course, is also subject to what is allowable under state law.

Inclusionary zoning ordinances can not only be a source of affordable housing but also result in a spreading of the housing units and reduction of the stigma of such housing. While living in Cherry Hill, I owned a townhouse in a project of 365 homes that included 36 affordable housing units. Although these units were smaller than the nonregulated homes, they were not identifiable as affordable homes and a lot of residents did not actually know they were even price controlled and occupied by those who could not afford the market rate homes.

This approach worked very well for Cherry Hill. There is no doubt that it was easier to get the ordinance adopted there because of the strong state mandate to provide affordable housing but could also work in other locations where housing affordability is a big issue. As valuable as this tool can be, I do not want to understate the controversy that can accompany such an approach.

Gentrification

Over the decades of redeveloping neighborhoods throughout the country, there have been great success stories of turning rundown areas into shining examples of vibrant, attractive environments. But what has that meant for the residents who lived in those areas that were priced out of the market and forced out of their homes? While the homes may have been inadequate according to housing code standards and what city council desires, they were homes that provided shelter and a community for residents who subsequently may have struggled to find any housing they could afford. New housing projects subsidized by federal funding do require the relocation of displaced tenants into housing that is affordable to them. However, the reality is that this does put a squeeze on the availability of affordable housing in a community. Additionally, some people in the community may have been paying next to nothing and could not afford even the lowest of rents in other units.

The Urban Displacement Project defines gentrification as (Urban Displacement Project n.d.)

a process of neighborhood change that includes economic change in a historically disinvested neighborhood by means of real estate investment and new higher-income residents moving in as well as demographic change, not only in terms of income level, but also in terms of changes in the education level or racial make-up of residents.

The negative consequences of gentrification present a great dilemma for cities. Parts of most cities are quite deteriorated and present crime and health issues. Improving those conditions is seen as highly desirable. But improving the physical conditions results in displacing the existing residents, councils need to ask themselves how valuable is that "improvement." Of course, the real question is how can the impact of improving the conditions in a neighborhood be minimized for the existing residents?

Despite the challenges that neighborhood redevelopment brings, I believe that it should be a goal of cities. In order to address the problems that gentrification can bring and not only improve the physical conditions of the area but also enhance the lives of the existing residents, I recommend that the city take an approach that will accommodate all the existing residents and newcomers and help the existing residents to compete for market rate housing. More specifically, the following strategies are recommended (Urban Displacement Project n.d.):

- Work in tandem with local nonprofit housing fund and community development corporations and developers to provide replacement housing for existing residents at a price that they can afford.
- Partner with the local nonprofits to provide housing as a last resort for those who can afford very little.
- Utilize increased density, where appropriate, to allow for existing residents to remain in the community and still accommodate newcomers.
- Institute an outreach effort to provide existing neighborhood residents with skill sets that will give them an opportunity to successfully compete for jobs, which will increase their economic well-being (relates to the social justice recommendations).
- Provide social services, which will enhance the life skills of existing residents, which will assist them in being successful in the local socio-economic setting (consistent with the social justice recommendations).

Homelessness

The reader is likely to feel that this chapter is moving from very challenging housing issues to the most intractable problems. While there
has been a homeless population issue in the United States for decades,
it certainly appears that this issue continues to be one of the most difficult to address. In 2020, the homeless count in this country was 580,466
people (National Alliance to End Homeless n.d.). Although this is less
than it was in 2007, it has increased over the past few years. There are a
number of causes that have been cited for homelessness. I believe that the
deinstitutionalization of the mentally ill has reduced the places where
they have to live as well as get some form of mental health assistance.
In addition, the increased cost of housing in major urban areas has
priced many out of the market. The rise in drug and alcohol addiction
has driven many into homelessness as they struggle to participate in
a normal work culture. In addition, domestic violence has often been
cited as an important cause as well for people who seek to get out of
abusive environments. Certainly, the loss of a job or the ability to pay
for housing costs is a significant issue.

Over the years, many cities and counties have claimed that other
places actually buy bus tickets to send some of the homeless population
to their city. While it is not clear how much of this takes place, I have
actually seen evidence that this has happened. It also seems evident that
the cities and counties that provide the best benefits for the homeless
attract other homeless people to come to their city. It does appear that
this happens for some in search of employment as well as better shelter
or food support. Many on the receiving cities say that providing good
benefits for the homeless just attracts a larger homeless population. So
while many have good intentions to help the homeless, they may feel a
disincentive to do so.

In the Seattle metropolitan area where I live, it is abundantly clear
that homelessness is a crisis that the City of Seattle struggles with,
and the City has not made a lot of apparent progress. One of the
manifestations of this is the proliferation of homeless encampments
in parks and public rights of way. This has led to many issues for the
community such as crime and health problems. The encampments in
themselves create a great dilemma. They are a tremendous detriment to
the city and neighborhoods where they exist, but they are also the only
shelter option for some people.

Many smart people have sought answers to the homeless dilemma.
My review of their work and my experience with the issue lead me

to the following recommendations. In partnership with the nonprofit providers, these are the best steps to address the issue.

- Cities and counties should provide support for food banks that feed the homeless and those who cannot afford to buy sufficient food.
- While cities and counties should continue to support emergency shelters, they should focus on providing permanent shelter for the homeless.
- Cities and counties need to provide the social services support in order to address alcohol and mental health problems.
- Local governments should not allow homeless encampments in parks and along public rights of way.

Foodbanks and church programs do a great service in providing food to the homeless. As this book is being written, they have been inundated due to the economic consequences of the COVID-19 pandemic. However, this should turn around with the vaccines that have been produced and the recovery of the economy. Local governments can leverage the private sector contributions by providing their own funding.

In most communities, there are substantial emergency shelter opportunities for the homeless, particularly during the cold winter months in the harsher climates. Governmental support for these is important but does not need to take a large amount of resources. The biggest contributions must go toward building housing that can shelter those who cannot afford housing. This housing can provide just the very basics for shelter and should be rather small. There are an increasing number of modular systems that can meet this need at a much more reasonable cost than traditional housing options. They generally are the scale of what is being called tiny houses.

In order to address the issue of attracting more and more homeless to a community, cities need to establish a list of existing homeless who are eligible to receive this housing. The city should provide permanent housing to those who sign up first. Once that group is housed, the city can move on to others who sign up after the first group. While the homeless are indeed suspicious of identifying themselves, the opportunity to live in a tiny house does offer a nice incentive. This incentive needs to be combined with the actions taken to eliminate encampments as an option for them.

Addressing the addiction and mental health issues of many homeless persons is vital to their well-being and to provide an opportunity for them to become self-supporting individuals. Indeed, many have excellent skills and could be gainfully employed if their mental health and addiction issues were resolved.

It is doubtful that we will solve all our homeless issues any time soon, but we can make a huge difference by pursuing these strategies. It will certainly take a commitment and substantial resources to make that critical difference.

As we examine the major issues in our cities and counties, another highly visible and important concern is the transportation system, which is part of the lifeblood for communities. Transportation is the subject of the following chapter.

References

National Alliance to End Homelessness. n.d. "State of Homelessness: 2021 Edition". Accessed August 20, 2021. https://endhomelessness.org/ homelessness-in-america/homelessness-statistics/state-of-homelessness-2021/

Urban Displacement Project. n.d. "Gentrification Explained". Accessed August 20, 2021. www.urbandisplacement.org/gentrification-explained

6 Transportation

Since everyone uses the transportation system in a community and it is so vital to get to jobs and other activities and many people spend a great deal of time and money on transportation, people generally have pretty strong opinions about it. Transportation in many ways serves as the lifeblood of the city. One has to just look at history and how access to transportation served as the basis for where settlements were located. Before the advent of modern modes of transportation, being next to water bodies, be it oceans, lakes or rivers, drove the development of the larger settlements. As rail transportation developed, locating along a rail line was vitally important. Rails gave way to the interstate highway system in driving the development of urban areas. Major airports have also played an important role in the development of cities. One can look at how the development of the Dallas Fort Worth Metroplex has been influenced by one of the most important airports in the country. Atlanta Hartsfield Airport, at times the world's busiest, has played a significant role in the development the Atlanta region. This chapter will examine the entire range of the transportation systems in urban areas throughout the United States, including all modes of urban transportation.

Transportation planning

The planning, funding, design and construction of transportation facilities are among the most critically important activities for a region. I use the term *region* because that is the scale at which the most significant transportation decisions are made. Transportation planning as well as most of the major funding decisions, including the use of federal and state transportation monies, is done by the metropolitan transportation planning agencies referred to as *Transportation Planning Organizations* (TPO). The designation was referred to as Metropolitan Planning

DOI: 10.4324/9781003262756-7

Organizations (MPO) when I was the Executive Director of the regional organization for the Metropolitan Phoenix area.

The chapter on Intergovernmental Relations will get into the structure of regional governance and recommendations for the best approach. However, the critical message that will be repeated in that chapter must be said here for emphasis that city and county managers and other leaders must be active participants in the regional planning efforts. The regional transportation planning process is often *the* place where decisions are made on what facilities are planned and funded in each locality. In fact, expenditures for *any* significant transportation investment *must* be in the Transportation Improvement Program (TIP) approved by the TPO for funding to be used for the project.

One other aspect of the regional planning process must be mentioned here as well. It is, unfortunately, most often that the transportation planning and facility decision process is not closely related to land use planning or the planning for other public facilities. It is up to the cities and counties to make this critical linkage in their comprehensive planning and capital improvement planning processes. This linkage will also help to build the case for these projects to be planned and funded at the regional level. In addition, decisions that are made at the regional level need to be done through the lens of the city's goals, particularly, the desired environmental and development patterns as well as meeting social justice concerns.

Finally, transportation planning and funding decisions need to be made on the basis of people's mobility and not the need to move cars. This ensures that adequate consideration is given to all modes of transportation, including public transit, pedestrian and bicycles.

In most US cities, the automobile is the principal means of getting around and will remain so for the foreseeable future. The value that people attribute to the freedom of movement and personal space is engrained in the culture of the country. However, there certainly has been some change in this view by many younger folks who see the personal freedom provided by an excellent public transit system to be more desirable. In the more dense cities that are served by effective public transit, many are electing to not own automobiles and use transit. Their mobility is enhanced by facilities that accommodate pedestrian and bicycle travel.

Back in the 1980s when often commuting to and from work by running, I was certainly in a very small minority of the population. While this is still relatively uncommon, there are a lot more people commuting by bicycle than many years ago. Of course, this is very common in other areas of the world. Even in the harsh weather conditions of Montreal,

Canada, there are protected bicycle lanes on downtown streets that have a rush hour at the close of the day. In many European cities, bicycle travel makes up a large portion of the commuting public. In many very large cities, public transportation is the overwhelming mode of travel.

Automobile travel

Despite the popularity of other modes of transportation, the automobile will continue to dominate the US landscape. There are some important considerations that managers should hold on to as their communities design and build roads and highways. Even though automobile travel is dominant, managers need to not lose sight of the other modes and the benefits they bring. The environmental cost of automobile usage is very high and the more that people travel on foot or by bicycle and transit, the less greenhouse gases will be produced.

Additionally, when considering the level of investment in alternate modes, one should consider the true and full cost of how much automobiles are subsidized through the tremendous investment in our road systems and parking facilities. Any cost comparison needs to take into account the full public cost of each mode of travel.

There also needs to be the recognition that in congested urban areas, it is virtually impossible to construct enough roads to build your way out of traffic congestion. Cities can make temporary improvements to the flow of traffic but, it is, most often, only temporary as the cars will increase to fill up the added capacity.

Finally, city leaders need to make sure that they are building facilities for automobiles to move people and not to serve the automobile.

Public transit

For decades, public transit has provided our urban centers with the means to efficiently move large numbers of people. In the densest cities, this has meant subways, elevated and at grade rail lines. It has also meant extensive bus systems, some of which have been assisted by exclusive lanes and queue jumping
opportunities. I have been involved in the planning, funding, design and construction of all the different types of public transit. While there are advocates for each type of mode of transit, city leaders need to make transportation planning, funding and design decisions based on the mode and layout that is most appropriate for their area. There are light rail advocates who will not be willing to consider bus systems that are much more suited to the characteristics and needs for a community.

Alternatively, there are some fiscal conservatives who will never support a light rail system, even in the densest environment. Careful analysis of the cost and benefits of different options *will* lead to the bet decisions but only if the city leaders *listen* to the professionals and make the most cost-effective selection.

Additionally, decisions to build major public transit facilities need to be viewed as long-term investments that will not only serve the community for decades but also shape the growth and development of the city. I remember back in 1973 when I was in undergraduate school at NC State going on an educational trip to Washington, DC, to look at the metro transit system that was under construction at the time. It had been in the planning, design and construction stage for many years. The first station was opened in 1976 to coincide with the 200th-year anniversary celebration of our country. This was a huge investment. The original cost was put at about $2.5 billion but had more than doubled by that time. It soared way past that figure. And they are still adding on to the system, which is currently well over 100 miles of railway. However, as expensive as it was, for many who live or travel to DC, it is hard to imagine the nation's capital without this rail system. In 2018, there were almost 300 million trips!

Another project will also serve to illustrate both building an appropriate solution and investing in the future. While working for the City of Seattle in the 1980s, I had some involvement in a project to build a transit tunnel under the downtown to accommodate the large amount of bus traffic that was clogging up the downtown streets. It was envisioned at the time that the tunnel would later be used for rail lines when the city took that step up to this higher capacity transit. At the time, the city had an all bus system that served the community very well. In fact, a majority of people commuting to the downtown to work used the bus system.

As Seattle experienced an amazing amount of growth, increasing its population from less than 500,000 when I was working for the city to more than 750,000 today, the tunnel now accommodates a light rail line going through the downtown. The city is in the process of building the largest number of new light rail lines of any city in the country. While the all bus system was ok decades ago, the light rail and bus system is needed today and in the future. Currently underway is the construction of an additional 58 miles of light rail at a cost in excess of $50 billion. Figure 6.1 shows a light rail station under construction in the City of Seattle.

I was also engaged in a very similar situation in the Minneapolis Metropolitan Area when I served as the Hennepin County Administrator

Figure 6.1 A light rail station under construction in the City of Seattle
photographed by the author.

during the mid-1990s. The area had a very robust bus system that
included some exclusive lanes and cue jumps. Similar to Seattle, more
than 50% of the commuters traveled to downtown via the bus system.
However, the area was growing and planning for moving toward light
rail system. The county was acquiring rights of way to accommodate future rail lines. Building of that system is currently underway to
supplement the bus system. The downtowns of both Minneapolis and
Seattle have very large employment bases and can fully justify a high-
capacity transit system like light rail.

When serving as the Executive Director of the Maricopa Association
of Governments (Phoenix Metro Area), I served as the Director of the
MPO. During my tenure, we planned and achieved funding for the first
light rail line for the area. This line ran through a section of the Cities
of Phoenix and Tempe and into the City of Mesa. While Phoenix and
Tempe do have a substantial amount of activity in their downtowns,
there is no concentration of employment. The initial light rail line runs
from the northern portion of the more historical part of the Phoenix
into the downtown, then on to the heart of Tempe and the mammoth

Arizona State University and continues into the heart of Mesa. Even with the activity along its route, it was a challenge to project adequate demand to justify the system. We did show that it would be a good investment and were able to obtain federal matching construction funding. This worked, in part, due to a dedicated portion of a local option sales tax.

Bus rapid transit

While traditional or light rail systems can be terrific solutions for some dense urban environments, bus systems, particularly those utilizing a bus rapid transit (BRT) concept, can be much more appropriate and cost effective. BRT systems utilize specially configured buses that travel principally along an exclusive right of way with stops only at stations where they load and unload level with station platform and collect fares. With the quick loading and unloading, if they operate on exclusive rights of way, these systems can achieve faster operating speeds than some light rail systems that operate in the road rights of way. These systems are also much less costly to build. *The Journalist's Resource*, in an online publication of the Harvard Kennedy School, *Bus versus rail: Costs, capacities and impacts*, cited a study by the University of Texas that found that the average cost of a BRT system was way less than one-half of a light rail system and less than one-tenth of the cost of traditional metro rail. Because of these advantages, many cities are choosing BRT as preferred options to accommodate a higher demand than what only traditional bus systems can deliver.

In both of the last two cities in which I managed, BRT systems would serve as a great addition to the traditional bus systems operating there. I advocated for proposals for building BRT lines in both cites although they have, at least as of yet, not been realized. In Greenville, there is an old abandoned rail right of way that runs from the edge of downtown out toward a very developed part of the city, somewhat parallel to a major thoroughfare. There is very little conflict with other roadways since this was built as a separate rail line. My approach was to position the publicly owned right of way as a significant portion of the local contribution for the project. Since the right of way is available and has little conflicts, the cost of building a BRT line would be very manageable. I also believed that BRT technology and the required level of investment would be appropriate for the city. While Greenville has a terrific downtown that people really enjoy visiting, the density of employment is not sufficient to justify the cost of a rail line. The city is considering alternative technologies for a transit facility along this corridor.

A somewhat similar situation exists in the City of Newport News. However, it is even a better set up for a major BRT line. The city is very long and has major roadways running in the roughly north-south linear configuration of the city. At the southern point of this spine is Newport News Ship Building, where all of the country's nuclear aircraft carriers are built and much of the nuclear submarines are contructed and at least 30,000 are employed. It is also near the historical downtown with many governmental offices. There is a rail line as well as a major water line running nearby one of these major roadways. While it is probably not feasible to build a rail line along a water line right of way, one could pave over it for a BRT line. Additionally, the densities of the city would make the cost of a rail line infeasible. Since most of the potential right of way is owned by the city, it could, like in Greenville, serve as a local contribution to match federal funding. The regional transit agency has undertaken a study and identified a BRT line running along this alignment as one of the alternatives for going forward.

These examples from both Greenville and Newport News illustrate some critical things to consider when looking to build a major transit facility. These include the following.

- Look for an appropriate technology to serve the needs of a community at a cost that is affordable and can be supported by the community.
- Plan for a system that serves the major needs of the city and region such as commuting to a relatively dense employment base.
- Attempt to use available assets and right of way to accommodate an exclusive and grade-separated travelway.
- Look for ways to come up with a local share to match state and federal funding.

Whatever type of transit system a community has or is planning to build, the most critical issue more than likely is funding for building new components of the system and its operation. Contrary to what some lay persons may believe, transit systems will never generate sufficient revenue to pay for even half of their operating costs and funding for system expansion costs have to be acquired on top of operating expenses. Whether it is a regional system serving a multicity and county area or just a citywide system, those entities that rely primarily on annual, general fund appropriations from their local governments always struggle to maintain sufficient funding. I have not seen a single very successful transit system in the United States that does not have some dedicated funding source. Dedicated funding sources include revenue streams such as a portion of the local sales tax or gas tax, an income tax or some other source of earmarked funding that goes to the transit system each year.

Systems that rely on annual appropriations from local governments compete with other needs of the city that may be judged to be a higher priority than transit. This was certainly the case when I assumed the position as City Manager for Greenville. While the operating subsidies provided by the federal government were eliminated well before I arrived in Greenville in early 2004, the countywide transit system had still received an operating subsidy the federal government provided to those transit systems serving a population less than 200,000 people. However, with the growth of the area, the system lost this operating subsidy and was operating at a deficit. In fact, the situation was so dire that it was faced with failing altogether. Realizing this, we put a plan together for the city to take over the system operations and utilize some operating efficiencies to put it on a sustainable path. The system was rebranded, and new and improved operation with on-time performance was rolled out. While this has been successful and the public funding has been somewhat increased, the system is still stymied by the lack of a dedicated funding source.

In the study of Nashville, which is referenced earlier, we looked at the transit systems in Nashville and the peer cities examined. It was an inescapable conclusion that the cities that had a dedicated funding source had a much more successful transit system and it was not even close.

Trail systems

Whether you live in an urban or rural area or whether it is a developing community or well-established place, facilities for pedestrian and bicycle travel are increasingly important. They are valuable for basic transportation as well as recreation. Urban and rural trail systems are critical to the quality of life in a community as well as important for economic development. Throughout my entire career, I have been engaged in helping to build trail systems. This includes systems in Tulsa, Seattle, Hennepin County, Greenville and Newport News as well as many others as a consultant. Some will see this as a self-serving pursuit for me since I have been such an avid runner and user of many of the trails I helped construct.

In Seattle in the 1980s, I was engaged with a very early rails to trails project. According to the Rails to Trails Conservancy, the conversions of abandoned rail lines have been a source of close to 25,000 of miles of trails throughout the United States. The rights of way for many rail lines was granted specifically for transportation purposes. Legislation passed by the US Congress declared trails to be a transportation purpose and that the rights of right established by railroads can be maintained for trails purposes. Otherwise, the rights of way could have reverted back to owners of the underlying property rights. Communities that have rail lines need to make sure to take advantage of any such opportunity that exists in their jurisdiction. Figure 6.2 shows a section of the Burke Gilman Trail in Seattle.

In building trails, it is important to look at regional systems and plan cooperatively with other locations. Connecting into trails in other local-ities can greatly enhance the desirability of any community's trails. The trail system in Greenville is a great example of this. The system started with the City building of a 5-mile section in the City of Greenville when I was the city manager. Working with the county, this was extended to close to a 30-mile system that leads into and out of the downtown core. It is also a terrific example of the value of trails for economic develop-ment. The trail has provided an impetus to the development of cafes,

Figure 6.2 A section of the Burke Gilman Trail in Seattle photographed by the author.

Figure 6.3 A portion of the Swamp Rabbit Trail in Greenville photographed
    by the author.

bike shops, boutique hotels and more. Figure 6.3 shows a portion of the
Swamp Rabbit Trail in Greenville, SC.

While the transportation system discussed in this chapter is often the
most visible and debated piece of the public infrastructure, there are
many other components that are also critically important. These will be
taken up in the next chapter.

7 Public facilities/infrastructure

This chapter covers many pieces of the urban infrastructure, which are indeed less visible even though they are vital to the functioning of our cities. These include water, wastewater, storm drainage and solid waste services. It will also include the more visible and popular parks and recreation services as well as public buildings. Of course, this will not be your primer for understanding all there is to know about these facilities, but it will cover some important considerations managers need to be engaged with and recommendations for addressing important issues. As each of these services is discussed, please bear in mind the role that they play in shaping the development of our urban areas.

Water

The availability of water has been particularly important for guiding the growth in some urban areas. While development in more rural areas most often has relied on wells for the potable water to support residences and other development, more urban densities require a centralized water system with supply, treatment and distribution facilities. Ensuring that there is sufficient water available is an important adequate public facilities test that managers need to make sure is part of the city's development review process.

Managers also need to be engaged in the rate-setting process, which is a principal focus of the water system discussion. While rate setting can be a very involved process, this discussion will stick to some basic considerations. Most rate structures generally include a base and variable rate. The base rate or fixed rate is the portion of the fee that everyone pays, which does not vary with the amount of water used. The variable rate is the charge based on the amount of water usage. Base rates are sometimes considered to be the charge that is used to pay for the infrastructure for the system, and the variable rate is used to pay for

DOI: 10.4324/9781003262756-8

the operation of the system. This is certainly not consistent throughout the water systems. What is particularly important to consider is that the base rate is vitally important for the stability of the system. In recent history, there has been a substantial reduction in the amount of water consumption per residence as well as for certain industrial and commercial users due to water conservation measures. Water systems that had relied principally on a variable rate saw significant drops in projected revenue leading to financial difficulties. It is critical for base rates to be an important part of the rate system.

Often, water systems are regional in nature and serve an area larger than a single city. The setting of rates can be a bit more complicated if the entity is city owned and operated yet functions as a regional system. This is fairly common in many urban areas. I have twice served as a manager where this situation exists. In Greenville, the system is technically a city entity but has a separate operational authority. In Newport News, the water system is a part of the city structure and is a city department. In both Greenville and Newport News, the water system charges a different rate for those customers in the city and those who are outside it. While this is based on the idea that it costs more to serve the outside customers and the city at one time paid nonwater system money for building the original in-city system. On the other hand, the jurisdictions outside the city often feel that the differential rate is much higher than is justified. In those circumstances, there needs to be a rational nexus between what are truly the additional costs to the system and the higher rates that those outside the city pay.

Since many water systems have historically generated more revenue than has been required to operate the system, cities have transferred water system revenue to the city's general fund. This has often gone beyond the amount that could be justified based on the potential water system overhead expenses the city incurs. In many jurisdictions, this extra amount has been in millions of dollars. Some states restrict the amount of extra revenue that the city can obtain. Having been in the position of a city manager who needs to balance an annual budget, I know how tempting it is to transfer additional revenue from the water system. All I can say is to resist that temptation. Enterprise funds like water systems are not intended to be used as cash cows for the city.

Environmental concerns are also important considerations for water systems. Those concerns can cover many issues, but I just want to focus on one that challenges many systems that are particularly dependent on aquifers for their supply. The continual withdrawal of a large amount of groundwater is a threat to many urban areas. This issue will be discussed later in this chapter.

Wastewater

Just as the availability of water service has driven the shape and form of development, the provision of wastewater systems has also been critical for development in some locations. While rural areas generally develop on septic systems, denser urban areas must rely on centralized sewer systems with collections lines and wastewater treatment.

Without going into a detailed discussion of wastewater systems, there are some issues to highlight. The sizing of collection system lines is a significant concern. This is also true for water distribution lines but will only be described in this section as the concerns are similar. When planning for the location and size of sewer lines, communities must take into consideration the demand based on the ultimate build out of the service area. To many, I am sure this seems obvious, but I am amazed how often this does not happen. You will recall the importance that was placed on the integration of land use planning with infrastructure planning. In addition, as areas of a city are redeveloped for more intensive uses, do not assume that the capacity of water and wastewater lines will be sufficient to accommodate the higher level of use.

Very often, permitting issues dominate a discussion on wastewater. The allowed capacities are generally quite tightly controlled by state-level permitting agencies. While the capacity of a system may seem to be a relatively straightforward issue, a frequent complicating factor in many jurisdictions is the amount of infiltration and inflow that may be occurring. Infiltration occurs when water gets into the pipes through faulty joints. At times, people may have made inappropriate connections to the sewer system to drain a basement or some other purpose. The extra water that goes into the system through these connections is referred to as inflow. There are instances where the infiltration and inflow can dramatically increase the flow to a treatment facility. I have seen instances where the wet weather flow can be three times the flow in dry conditions. This greatly restricts the capacity for a plant and the amount of development that can be permitted. So programs to control the infiltration and inflow can be critical for a city. Reducing this extra water getting into the sewer can save millions in plant capacity upgrades.

When available capacity in a wastewater treatment plant is limited and communities are restricted in the amount of development that can be permitted, it is critical for the city to have a tracking system to determine not only the amount of existing flow but also the amount of flow that has already been permitted. I have been amazed by the number of jurisdictions that do not do this properly.

One of the major issues that have been critical for wastewater systems has been the disposal of treated effluent. The level of required treatment has dramatically increased since the time that sewer outfalls deposited effluent just a step up from raw sewerage. Even today, with a very high level of treatment, disposal of effluent is a major concern. However, it also presents a significant opportunity. While water bodies cover about 71% of the earth's surface and water is, obviously, very plentiful, over 96% of the water on the earth is salt water in oceans. Programs to use effluent for nonpotable water needs, such as watering golf courses, have been in place for decades. Many urban areas are strapped for clean water for household consumption among other needs for potable water. For many years, reclaiming water from wastewater treatment plants has been studied and put into practice on a limited basis. Discharges from treatment plants have gone into lakes, which are the source of raw water for water treatment plants.

A program led by the Hampton Roads Sanitation District (HRSD) looks to inject highly treated effluent into the aquifer that is a major source of drinking water for the region of southeast Virginia. In addition to replenishing the aquifer, which is showing signs of depletion, this program can help to address the ground subsidence and saltwater intrusion issues that are affecting the area. Managers need to be aware of and engaged in the state-of-the-art use of effluent and advocate for similar programs that will assist their cities to be assured of adequate water resources. If this was not self-evident, it has been made most abundantly clear as the Virginia Commonwealth agency, which issues permits for local ground water withdrawals, has started to reduce allowable withdrawals due, at least in part, to groundwater subsidence and saltwater intrusion. More on the HRSD programs related to wastewater treatment will be described in the intergovernmental relations chapter.

Stormwater

Issues relating to stormwater have gained great complexity and importance in the past decade. While the roots of these developments originate from the Clean Water Act in 1972, it was not until a court ruling definitively stated that the act mandated that pollution from stormwater runoff be regulated as well as the point source outfalls into water bodies. It has taken many decades for the control of stormwater runoff to be fully implemented. However, the requirements of the National Pollution Discharge Elimination System (NPDES) regulate stormwater. The permit requirement for stormwater includes the quantity and quality of storm drainage. The permit requirements are particularly rigorous where areas drain into more sensitive bodies of water. The complexities are beyond the scope of this book, but managers need to familiarize themselves with the requirements and implications for their jurisdictions.

Not only has permitting to control water quality increased dramatically but so has control of the quantity of runoff. The more developed an area, the more critical these regulations are because of the impervious surfaces that increase the amount and speed of urban runoff. While controls on new development have been ramped up considerably, most places must ensure that developments create no greater level of runoff than before the development occurred and the amount that is allowed does not leave the site any faster.

Even with these updated regulations constraining the flow of water, cities have to deal with many instances of flooding and must address significant problems for their communities. The requirements to treat the quality of runoff, combined with the cost to maintain drainage facilities, put a significant financial burden on city budgets. Many local governments have instituted a fee to fund a stormwater utility to pay for these costs. Some may see this fee as just another tax that adds to the community's burden. Technically, it is not a tax and ought to be viewed in the same light as water and wastewater fees. It is a critical resource that is a virtual necessity for funding city operations.

Stormwater fees are generally based on the amount of area of a property. Most often, a system of calculating the fee is based on the size of a typical single-family lot and is some multiple of that typical single-family lot area, referred to as an equivalent residential unit or ERU. Thus, the amount that a commercial building would pay would be some number of ERUs. Since all properties, regardless of their use, have rainwater falling on them, no properties are usually exempt. There is often a push from tax exempt property to exclude them from the fee, but that is not appropriate as it is a user-based fee and not a tax. It becomes a very slippery slope to start exempting anyone. That goes for public entities as well such as the city itself that may be charging the fee. Some locations do allow exemptions or reductions based on certain actions such as utilizing a rain garden that retains and reuses rainfall.

Solid waste

Obviously, dealing with garbage and trash pickup and disposal is an important urban service with high citizen expectations. Getting that wrong has been a great grief for managers and elected officials. This even includes a timely pickup of leaves in the fall. Solid waste handling also has significant implications for the environment. The difference between a state-of-the-art solid waste program with aggressive recycling and composting and a trash only collection system is huge. Local governments need to fund and operate quality solid waste programs. While there are challenges in marketing or even giving recycled material away, recycling programs are abundant and popular with citizens who understand its importance. Composting is much less common but is gaining ground in acceptance. Places like Seattle where I lived in the 1980s had composting efforts at the time. These programs are much more rigorous today and are more widely used. Managers need to put in place efforts to demonstrate the value of both recycling and composting not only to save space in their landfills but also to reuse materials.

The funding of solid waste collection and disposal is generally paid for by user fees, although this is not true in a number of areas. For instance, the property tax has historically been used in most South Carolina localities. When I began as the Greenville City Manager, they had only a minimal monthly charge of $2.50 that had been put in place to start a recycling program. Over time, I worked with the city council to increase this fee to come close to a full cost recovery. The gradual increase was vital to the city council acceptance of this effort. I believe that a full cost recovery through solid waste fees should be the goal of communities.

A fully functioning solid waste enterprise system, in addition to taking pressure off the property tax system, can assist in reducing the waste that goes to the landfill and can increase recycling. This can be done by using a variable rate that charges customers based on the size of their trash can. The smaller the can, the less they pay and the less they send to the landfill.

While it may appear relatively straight forward, solid waste funding can get fairly complex. When I assumed the Hennepin County Administrator position, the County was operating a large trash incinerator. At that time, the county controlled the waste stream. That is, it was able to require all haulers in the county within its 45 cities to bring waste to the incinerator. Shortly into my tenure with the county, the US Supreme Court ruled that jurisdictions like Hennepin could not control the waste stream throughout the county. This led many jurisdictions to bring their trash to landfill operations outside the county and even outside the state where the tipping fee (fee charge for dumping waste) was much lower than that of the county with its expensive incinerator operation. We were able to reduce the tipping fee substantially but could not compete with the landfills.

In order to address this, we instituted a flat fee for every household in the county, which was used to subsidize the incinerator operation and bring the tipping fee into a competitive position. This basically operated similar to the base charge in a water system.

Parks and recreation

While parks and recreation facilities and services have always been popular in communities, they have more recently taken on an even greater level of importance. When people make a decision about where to live, parks and recreation are sometimes at the very heart of the considerations that they make. I will focus on just one aspect that is very different today. People are looking for an interconnected open space network with paths and recreational opportunities connected to this network. Cities all over the country have recognized this and are responding by building a web of linear open space throughout their communities. The best time to start to build this network is when development occurs. This means ensuring that development ordinances require that links in the system are built. However, for any community the time is now. No one can afford to wait for years to get going. It only makes it that much more difficult.

When I arrived in Greenville as the City Manager in early 2004, the city was frankly way behind where it should have been in building an open space network. We were able to take advantage of some abandoned rail lines as described earlier and some available corridors along rivers and construct a well-used system. However, building the system has been harder and more expensive, and many great river corridor possibilities were shut off by existing development. So plan and fund this work immediately.

Setting levels of service

As I recommended earlier, communities should set standards for the level of service for public infrastructure and make sure that those levels are maintained as development occurs. This process needs to involve the city and county elected officials and engage the citizens. Their engagement will help build the interest and will provide the necessary funding to build and maintain these assets.

Public buildings

While there is certainly a multitude of concerns related to public buildings, this section will deal with just two important considerations that are not well understood or utilized: performance-based contracts and arc flash studies.

Performance-based contracts can be used by localities to help finance energy efficiency improvements to public buildings and other facilities. This process involves the city or county contracting with a private firm to make energy efficiency improvements and utilizing the savings in energy to fund the upgrades. These energy efficiency improvements could include replacing HVAC (heating, ventilation and air conditioning) systems, adding insulation and replacing lighting systems with those that are more energy efficient, among other measures.

This process generally begins with an energy efficiency audit to determine improvements that can be made and the amount of revenue that can be saved. If that audit shows sufficient revenue to justify the improvements, the locality then may issue a request for proposals for firms that might be willing to make the improvements for the revenue that can be gained by the savings. The city or county would then select the best proposal and enter into an agreement with them to do the improvements. These contracts can result in improvements running in many millions of dollars.

When I was working as the Newport News City Manager, the public works director recommended that I include money to conduct an "arc flash" study for the city. Having been convinced of the importance of doing this, we did fund and complete a study. A few years later while working for an engineering and consulting firm, I was surprised how many of our clients' managers did not even know what an arc flash study was. I am guessing that many of you may not be aware of this concern.

An arc flash is a situation that can be created from an electrical arc. This can occur through a contact with electrical systems or improper maintenance of equipment. This can cause an explosion to occur. This happens in the country several times every day. These explosions can cause injury or death to employees. The average cost of medical treatment for survivors will generally be more than a million dollars.

OSHA (Occupational Safety and Health Administration) regulations require employers to study and identify potential hazards and make improvements to correct the hazard. Localities that are found to be out of compliance can be subject to large fines, running into the hundreds of thousands of dollars. Every local government needs to address this issue if they have not done so.

Managers are sometimes challenged in getting councils to recognize the importance and value of investing in public infrastructure. It is often easier to get council's attention on economic development projects, which add jobs for a community as well as help build wealth. Of course, the amount of public funding that goes to economic development can be controversial, and not every project is going to be successful. These and other issues relating to economic development are dealt with in the next chapter.

8   Economic development

Economic development is indeed a very visible activity of cities and counties. The promise of many new jobs and an expansion of the tax base that comes with an announcement can be exciting to hear for citizens as well as the business community. Of course, there is a lot more to economic development than the splashy announcements of projects involving company relocations or expansions. In fact, an overwhelming amount of the economic growth in a community comes from the growth in small businesses. Also, there is a lot of work that goes into setting the stage for attracting and growing businesses. There are some key aspects of the economic development process that managers and city leaders should be knowledgeable of and involved with. These include knowing about some important tools that are available as well as being engaged in the terms of any project deals.

Economic development projects most often come with some incentives provided by the host city or county in addition to what the state may provide. These incentives could involve public expenditures for infrastructure, which is necessary for a project, or some form of tax breaks. A tax break could be provided based on things such as the amount of revenue that will be generated by a development or the number of new jobs that will be created. Managers not only need to know the details of these incentives but also need to ensure that a solid cost-benefit analysis is done and it shows that the community will indeed have a net benefit from its investment. This analysis should compare the amount of total investment by the community with the projected benefits and ensure that the benefits substantially outweigh the costs. Managers need to be assured that the project has a high likelihood of success and that there are safeguards in the event that the project proponents do not deliver as promised. There should be mechanisms in any development agreement to recoup, or "claw back" in the parlance of economic developers, any incentives that have been provided.

DOI: 10.4324/9781003262756-9

Tax increment financing

In my extensive economic development engagement in a number of communities, two tools have been critical for the success of projects. These are tax increment financing (TIF) and new market tax credits (NMTC). Both of these were utilized in the very successful redevelopment of the Greenville, SC, downtown. TIF involves the use of projected revenues from the incremental tax base that results from development. At least in theory, this is revenue that would not have happened but for the new development. In downtown Greenville, as in a lot of other places, this revenue has been used to build public infrastructure and amenities to support the new development. This included parking structures, streetscape improvements and utility upgrades. It is safe to say that this tool has made the highly regarded revitalization of Greenville possible.

Due to the success with downtown revitalization, a lot of cities sent delegations to Greenville to study its success while I was the manager. That has continued even up to this time. Many of the visitors came from North Carolina cities as they had found redeveloping their downtowns particularly challenging. Part of it is because they did not have the ability to utilize TIF districts to fund public facilities. The comparison of state enabling legislation between North Carolina and South Carolina was most interesting. Whereas the availability of doing TIF in South Carolina was a huge advantage to Greenville, their strict annexation laws greatly hindered the growth of the city compared with their North Carolina counterparts where much more liberal annexation laws existed. While Greenville has a vibrant employment base and a large daytime population of somewhere in the vicinity of 200,000, the number of residents is relatively small, at less than 70,000. I have always maintained that if Greenville, SC (there actually already is a Greenville, NC), were in North Carolina, it would have expanded its boundaries to include a population of at least 200,000 and probably close to 300,000. Since I left the city as its manager in 2010, the laws in both states have changed. North Carolina's annexation laws have made it more difficult to annex property but have provided more of an opportunity to create TIF districts.

The rules regarding TIF vary greatly from state to state, and there are many complexities that city leaders need to understand. For instance, in some places, the incremental tax revenues that can be used for development include those that would otherwise have flowed to not only the city but also other entities such as the county and school district. Other places restrict the revenues just to city tax increments. Also, the entities who need to approve of the use of TIF can vary, sometimes including all the entities whose tax revenue would be potentially used. Additionally, the allowed uses are different from state to state as are the procedures for using bonds in anticipation of the incremental revenues to pay for the public investment.

New market tax credits

While TIF can be complex, the rules and procedures involving NMTC are equally involved. NMTC are credits someone investing in a project gains for their federal income tax. This credit amounts to 39% of the investment. To qualify, the investment must be in a low-income area. Community development entities are provided an amount of tax credits from the federal government and allocate them to selected projects. While the rules are incredibly complex, the bottom line is that at least 20% of the cost of a project can be saved through the use of these tax credits.

According to the Tax Policy Center, an arm of the Urban Institute and Brookings Institution, since 2003, there has been $27 billion in tax credits. These credits have been gained through more than 5,300 projects (Tax Policy Center n.d.). During my past several years as the Greenville City Manager, virtually every project utilized NMTC.

In addition to the projects in downtown Greenville, I was personally involved in recommending and supporting the use of NMTC in the funding of a new school for my church. This was after I had left the city manager position and was working for Elliott Davis. I had also pushed the use of this program in Newport News when we were building a grocery store in an underserved community.

In December 2020, the tax credit program was extended for another five years at five billion dollars per year. So it will continue to be a very important program that managers need to be aware of and understand how it can be utilized to benefit projects in their community.

Job training

To mirror a phrase from the real estate industry, the three most important things about economic development for many citizens are jobs, jobs, jobs. While added revenue is certainly important to cities, people in the community want to see more jobs. However, expanded employment opportunities are more than just about the jobs that a business will bring to the area. For people in the community to be able to take advantage of available positions, they must have the required skill set. This often means that technical or other trainings need to be provided. Many times, companies relocating to the area can be attracted by such training programs, and other times, it may be an absolute requirement for their move to a community. As industries become more and more automated, this training is going to be more and more critical. Even in the mid-2010s when I was involved with recruiting a transmission manufacturer to the Greenville area, the company required more than one-half of the 1,300 people they were going to hire to be able to work at an intelligent workstation. Cities and counties must be actively engaged in helping to train residents for jobs that are available today and will be tomorrow.

One underutilized avenue for job training is apprentice programs. These can certainly range in the level of skills taught as well as their sophistication. The most amazing apprentice program I have seen is conducted by Newport News Shipbuilding. Their apprentice school includes a four- to five-year program that prepares people to become master shipbuilders. The highly competitive selection process leads to a program where the apprentices actually get paid as they learn their craft. Of course, programs do not need to be this involved and can be very focused on a specific set of immediate needs for a business. Local governments can partner with businesses and technical schools to assist with the development of apprentice programs or to offer other job-specific trainings.

Regional economic development agencies

Most economic development marketing is often done at a regional level. The reasons for this include the following.

- It is more economical to combine marketing resources for a joint effort of cities in a region.
- The available work force is based on the region and not individual cities.
- The subcontractor and supplier network that would support a business operation is, most often, regional in nature.
- The characteristics of an area that would attract businesses are regional in nature.
- The education and training availability is mostly regional.
- Business prospects see places as regions for the above reasons.
- Local businesses operate on more of a regional basis and see economic development that way as well.
- The economic development plans referred to a Comprehensive Economic Development Strategy (CEDS), which is necessary for a community to receive federal economic development funding, is developed at a regional level.

In addition to marketing, many regional economic development organizations are actively engaged in business recruitment along with and on behalf of the cities and counties in a region. Because of the important role of regional economic development entities, it is important for cities and their managers to be active participants in the regional economic development organizations.

While I have often been very engaged with regional economic development agencies as a city manager as well as while working with Elliott Davis, I was especially involved as the Newport News City Manager. The Hampton Roads Economic Development Alliance (HREDA) is the regional organization for the area. The alliance had been dominated by private sector business leaders since its beginning. Most of the cities in the region had very active individual economic development efforts, but the level of cooperation was significantly lacking because they were not as actively engaged in the regional organization as they should have been. In fact, the organization bylaws said that only private sector representatives could be elected to be chair of the board of directors. I was elected to the board and became an active supporter of economic development in the region, attending events and announcements in the various cities in the region. When the bylaws were changed, I became the first public sector chair of the board. I relate this story to emphasize that managers need to be very active participants as it will not only serve the regional interest but will also significantly benefit their cities. We need to recognize that regions are the economic entity and cities will benefit most when they are part of that regional program.

Marketing the city

In addition to working with the regional economic development program, there are other things that cities can do to market themselves. There are three examples I will use to illustrate this. The first is an opportunity I led in both Greenville and Newport News to have a section about each city in an airline magazine. In both Greenville and Newport News, I worked with the company that published the onboard magazine for US Airways to get a large section in a monthly issue dedicated to the city. In Newport News, this was a 40-page segment that exposed over five million passengers that month to the best assets of the city. In doing this for the cities, I was engaged in identifying stories as well as potential sponsors. While participating in fund raising is not a typical or traditional city manager activity, it provided outstanding benefits.

Active fund raising was also a key to a great event the City of Greenville hosted. Due to some good connections with the sport of cycling, we learned about a chance to bid to be the site for the US Pro Cycling Championships. Since I wrote about this in my first book, I will truncate the explanation here. We developed a bid and were successful in being the host city for the US Championships for seven years. One of the roles I served was to help raise $500,000 annually for sponsorships. The event brought annually over one million worldwide media exposures. This is a number that is still hard for me to wrap my mind around! As I explained in the first book, when we hosted a group of Canadian businessmen who were avid cyclists, it established a connection that led to TD Bank buying the failing Carolina First Bank and establishing a major regional hub and over 1,000 jobs in the city.

In addition, in Greenville we had two other particularly noteworthy events that helped to promote the city and tourism. Prior to my arrival in 2004, the city had sponsored an arts and crafts street festival over a long weekend. At that time, the organizers felt that the event needed a face lift. The decision was made with the approval of the city to suspend the event for a year and reinvent it. The event was recast as Artisphere, a high-level juried arts and crafts fair. The city provided a significant amount of upfront seed money to launch the festival, and substantial private donations were obtained. Artisphere quickly became one of the top art fairs in the country, drawing artists from not only the United States but also other countries. It generated tourism as well as helped to brand Greenville as a real up-and-coming city.

Artisphere was an anchor for the spring festivals in the city, and another signature event did the same for the fall. While the city had conducted a very large food and entertainment festival in the fall, it was largely a regional upstate South Carolina audience. In order to promote the growing restaurant scene in Greenville, a culinary and wine festival was created, which is now called Euphoria. While the city provided a substantial investment, an event champion was once again a key ingredient. Like Artisphere, Euphoria began a quick success and attracted people from all parts of the country.

A short story will help to illustrate the value of this type of event. The public and private sectors were most interested in attracting venture capital to the potential startup businesses. After Euphoria had grown in stature, the city, along with local businesses, hosted leaders of many of the country's major venture capital firms for the weekend and the festival. This was quite unusual because the firms really never had been drawn together like this before. During the weekend, the participants were introduced to many of the startups in the city. While there had already been an interest by one firm in a Greenville startup, this event solidified the commitment. This business, Proterra, is now a leading manufacturer of electric buses and batteries and employs many hundreds of people in the city. While I had left as the city manager by the time of the event, I participated with my private sector firm, Elliott Davis, who was a major sponsor for the weekend.

Finally, I am a big proponent of sister cities and the relationships that they may bring to promote a city. While I have participated in many sister cities events, none was more rewarding and important than when I served as the lead of a delegation visit to China. In the ten days we were in China, we visited eight cities and dozens of companies, many of which were interested in establishing locations in the United States. The planning for mega cities and redevelopment of older is quite incredible. The local infrastructure investment is particularly noteworthy. Figure 8.1 depicts a model of a massive city development project in China.

In addition, we learned a great deal about the tremendous investment in public infrastructure other levels of the Chinese government are making. The high-speed train network they are constructing

Figure 8.1 A model of a massive city development project in China photographed by the author.

across the country will be a long-term boon to their development. While the trains have the capability of approaching 300 miles per hour, they are operating at present at about 200 miles per hour. As of 2020, China had 24,000 miles of high-speed rail. The network is projected to grow to 43,000 miles by 2035. How many miles of high-speed rail does the United States have today? That would be zero miles of truly high-speed rail. Figure 8.2 shows a high-speed train at a station in China.

While local governments are not responsible for building high-speed rail lines, they need to be engaged if there is a proposal for a line that might serve their area. Due, in part, to having worked in somewhat large metropolitan areas, I have been engaged in the planning process for potential high-speed lines being planned in Florida, Minnesota, Arizona, South Carolina and Virginia. A manager's engagement could make the difference on the routing of a high-speed line or whether there would be a station location in your community. You can see by this that there is certainly a lot of potential activity around the country.

Figure 8.2 A high-speed train at a station in China photographed by the author.

Research parks

Earlier in the discussion on land use planning, I described the zoning case I became engaged with early on as the Newport News City Manager. Now, I would like to tell the "rest of the story" and focus on the importance of high-technology business. The major impetus for this development was the Jefferson National Laboratories (JLab) adjacent to this planned development. JLab is a research facility that studies the makeup of atomic matter. They have a particle accelerator that breaks up atoms into tiny component parts. I know, atoms are small to begin with! This facility is an incredible asset to the community with about 800 permanent employees, largely scientists. JLabs also houses well over 1,000 scientists from around the world who do research at the facility. The driving force behind the research and office space of this project was to benefit from the intellectual capital coming from the research conducted at JLab. The approximately one million square feet of space will add thousands of highly skilled and well-paying jobs to the city.

However, there is even a greater opportunity available. JLab is in competition with another national laboratory for the construction of an electron ion collider, which will allow for an even closer examination of atomic particle makeup. If JLab is awarded for this project by the US Department of Energy, it would bring a four billion dollar economic impact to the area and result in 4,000 jobs. This indeed has the opportunity to remake the local economy.

Another example of a major economic benefit from a research and office park is the Clemson University Center for Automotive Research in Greenville, SC. This facility is an outgrowth of the abundant automobile manufacturing in this area of South Carolina. Many of the local automobile–related manufacturers like BMW and Michelin have joined forces with the Clemson graduate school of automotive engineering to develop this center of research and development for the automobile industry. There are already several buildings and hundreds of jobs that are adding greatly to the local economy.

These are but two examples of higher technology making major contributions to the local economy. I am sure that everyone has seen this in different parts of the country. I have already mentioned the amazing amount of growth in the Seattle area. This was driven, in large part, by the tech industry. This is evident throughout the metropolitan area, which has grown tremendously in the last two decades. Amazon alone employs about 50,000 people in the city itself. Along with this great expansion of high-tech business has come a dramatic increase in the annual income of the city's residents. In 2019, the median family income was 56% higher than the national median. In that year, the city's married couples with a child younger than 18 years of age had a median family income exceeding $200,000. Of course, many other things have come along with this growth, like very heavy traffic congestion and housing costs that price many out of the market. The point is not to lavish praise on the city but rather to point out the value of high-tech businesses to drive economic development.

Economic impact studies

Many entities in a city play a valuable role in contributing not only to its quality of life but also to its economic well-being. In order to help identify the benefits, I have been a proponent of conducting economic benefit studies to quantify the economic contributions that the entities make to a city. I have participated in doing some of these studies as a consultant on behalf of cultural organizations. One such study showed the extensive economic impact the Peace Center for the Performing Arts in Greenville made to the local economy. They used this information to assist in their fundraising for a major improvement project of over 20 million dollars. So it is important to recognize that there are many entities that contribute significantly to the overall economic health of a community. Figure 8.3 is a picture of the Peace Center.

Figure 8.3 A picture of the Peace Center photographed by the author.

Entities that are critical to economic development most certainly include the educational system. The next chapter addresses this critical resource.

Reference

Tax Policy Center. n.d. "Briefing Book, Key Elements of the U.S Tax System". Accessed August 20, 2021. www.taxpolicycenter.org/briefing-book/what-new-markets-tax-credit-and-how-does-it-work

9 Education

The discussion on education will be limited to the ways that local governments generally are involved in the education system, although it will also include some issues that ought to be of great interest to a local government manager. This generally revolves around the funding for education but will also encompass other support for educating the community. This includes the growth and development of a university resource for the community.

Education funding

The responsibility for funding elementary and secondary education for a community varies greatly across the country. Schools generally utilize funding from local, state and federal sources. Some locations have fully independent school districts that determine their own local funding and even have the power to set the tax rates for education revenues. Conversely, some cities or counties not only set the local tax rates for education but also determine the local funding for schools. There are many hybrid arrangements as well. I have worked in cities and counties that are both ends of this dichotomy.

In the instances where the city or county determines the local contribution to school funding, it can frequently present a challenging situation for the city manager. It is quite natural for school boards and superintendents to push for the most funding that they will be able to obtain from city councils, which control the purse strings. I think it is fair to say that even in the most robust budget years, there will not be enough money to cover everything that schools would like to provide for students and teachers. In lean years, shortfalls become more critical. School boards and even sometimes superintendents can take the political route to obtain what they believe is the appropriate level of funding. The manager is faced with a great many competing demands

DOI: 10.4324/9781003262756-10

and must balance all the needs for funding local services, including the school system.

I certainly experienced this firsthand as the Newport News City Manager, where the city council determined the local financial contribution to the school district beyond the state mandated level that must be provided by the locality. Based on this and other experiences, my recommendations for sorting through this situation include the following.

- Meet with the superintendent early before any budgets are developed and openly layout the overall financial considerations going into the next budget.
- Obtain financial information from the school district, which shows their needs as well as other sources of projected revenue.
- Include considerations of funding for schools in the five-year financial projection and discussion of priorities for the city with the city council.
- Establish some form of metrics to evaluate the school funding needs and a way to compare schools' needs with the city operating departments' needs.
- Discuss the potential budget recommendations with the superintendent in a private meeting and the reason for the recommendations.
- Seek an agreement with the superintendent on the level of funding that will be appropriate for the schools.

The relationship between the city manager and the superintendent of schools is very important to making the budget process work well. This can be challenging when the school district is putting a lot of pressure on the superintendent to push hard for a big increase in financial support. However, the more the manager can establish an open and trusting relationship, the better the process will go. This is aided greatly when both parties can share detailed financial information. By including a discussion on school funding in the context of the long-term financial planning, the manager can get a reasonable understanding of where the schools fit into the council's priorities.

There will still need to be a basis for comparing the school's needs with those of city government departments. The biggest driver in the budget process will be personnel costs, so salary and benefit comparisons will be important. There certainly is value in making sure that the amount of raises over time is comparable. However, there will always be those who believe that teachers are underpaid. The same is likely to be true for some city departments such as the police. Given this dynamic, it is important to have regional data for the different types of positions to help place the salary needs based on competitiveness in the area.

In addition to personnel costs, schools can have a significant financial need for new schools, renovation of buildings and equipment purchases. Assessing these needs should be driven by an evaluation of long-term plans for upgrades and replacements. Agreeing on a plan over a number of years can serve as a guide to funding allocations. Of course, these plans need to be based on reasonable expectations for what will be available for funding.

I believe strongly that it is often difficult to have sensitive conversations with very many people in the room. There is a time when one-on-one meetings are the only way to achieve a frank dialog. A meeting with the school superintendent and city manager to discuss the budget realities and seek common ground can be vital. If both the school board and the council have a measure of confidence in the superintendent and the manager, they should be able to reach an agreement on funding for schools. If one of the boards lacks sufficient confidence or the superintendent and the manager do not have a trusting relationship, then decisions on school funding may have to play out on the public political stage. This also happens if the council or the school board is simply unwilling to see one another's perspective.

While cities, in some cases, may be responsible for the funding of education, does that mean that councils' have any say in what the money is spent on and how school business is conducted? Certainly, in some instances, funding decisions are not a lump sum payment to be spent any way the school district chooses and there is generally some designation of funds for some purposes. Even where this is not formally part of the process, there can be some expectations, such as agreeing to fund at a level so teachers can get a certain amount of raise. Councils can also set some other potential expectations. This might include funding such that each student has access to a personal computing device.

Like everyone else, council members have opinions about how school should be conducted. When a council controls the purse strings, there can be a tendency for at least some council members to want to tell the school district how to do their business. This is indeed a slippery slope and another potential sticky situation for the manager. I believe that any conversation about how the schools instruct students is best left between the council and the school board. If this happens at all, it should occur at a high policy level. Of course, the dynamic of this is very different if it is an elected school board versus one that is appointed by the council. I believe that any manager involvement ought to take the form of working with the school superintendent to set desired outcomes for the system and assisting in measuring and evaluating their success.

Technical/community college

In some instances, cities and counties also control a portion of funding that may go to technical or community colleges. In these instances, there is more often the ability of the local government to set some level of expectation of the programs that will be provided. If that opportunity exists, the two most important directions should be to ensure that there is technical training that prepares students to assume jobs that exist in the community and that they partner with four-year institutions to make a smooth transition from the community college to a full degree program.

In providing training that is specific to local industries, these schools need to be encouraged to partner with the businesses, so that they can guide the colleges in the type of coursework offered.

An urban university

The term *urban university* refers to a university that exists within an urban region that has a major focus on educating the students of that area. Urban universities generally serve not only traditional student populations closely following from high school to college but also older students who have been or still are in the work force. These non-traditional students may be looking to advance within the current field of employment or move to another profession. Many of these urban universities have grown to be quite large institutions by meeting this previously untapped need. While there is really no exact classification, I would say that George Mason, Towson State, Central Florida, Toledo and Illinois at Chicago, among many others, function, at least in part, as urban universities.

I have felt that having the presence of an urban university is virtually a prerequisite to achieving a robust and modern economy. I certainly felt this way while living in Greenville, SC. While the wonderful institution of Furman University was in the region, it was never going to capture the type of growth in student population and serve as this type of resource. Clemson University was just too far away and focused on more traditional students. The city did have a branch campus of the University of South Carolina Upstate (USC Upstate) that had great growth potential and could have an opportunity to fulfill this need. In fact, I felt so strongly about this that I almost took the position that was offered to be the Vice Chancellor of USC Upstate to run the Greenville campus and grow it into the type of facility necessary to meet Greenville's needs.

Just as the education is a critical need in a community, so is health care. It is important for not only local government employees but also the community as a whole. As I write this, we are in the midst of the country's and the world's worst pandemic in over a century. We are so much more aware of the importance health care plays in our lives. The next chapter will cover this topic.

10 Health care

This chapter will focus on the role that local government plays in health and not delve into the entire health care system and the complicated domain of federal health care policies and laws. This will include indigent health care, public health and employee health care.

Indigent care

Earlier, I mentioned that my responsibilities as the Hennepin County Administrator included oversight of the Hennepin County Medical Center, an HMO and large group of doctors. There are lots of issues that come with this type of facility but since they are not very typical of local governments, I will only talk about one which is related to the services cities and counties typically provide. As with all hospitals, particularly public hospitals, there is a significant amount of care that is not reimbursed, which is referred to as indigent health care. This is a care where the individuals do not have insurance or any other means to pay for the service they receive. Hennepin County is still today the largest provider of indigent health care in the State of Minnesota. Even as far back as the 1990s when we prepared the county's budget, I had to plan for tens of millions of dollars for indigent care each year. There are some hospitals in the country where this number now runs into the hundreds of millions of dollars. According to the American Hospital Association, since 2000, more than $660 billion of services have been received by patients who could not pay their bills.

Cities and counties typically see this same phenomenon if their responsibilities include emergency medical services (EMS). Much of this occurs for ambulance services when people who have no ability to pay for transportation to the hospital use ambulances as their ride to the hospital emergency room. It is often the same group of people who rely on this strategy to meet their health care needs. In essence, the hospital

DOI: 10.4324/9781003262756-11

emergency room is their primary care provider. In Newport News, we referred to this group as our frequent flyers. This is quite common throughout the country.

In order to address this, some communities are approaching this in partnership with the hospitals. I felt that if we partnered with the hospitals to find an alternate way to get the health care resources to the frequent flyers, we could pool the resources we would jointly save and still come out ahead. In addition, the residents would end up with a better option to meet their needs. In order to do this, some communities are finding ways to bring primary care to the homes of those who lack the resources to get care. This can be done through nurses making house calls as well as partnering with neighborhood health clinics to provide primary care. The subsidies provided by the city and hospitals will certainly be less than their cost for indigent care and nonpaying users of the city EMS.

Public health

Public health responsibilities most typically operate at a county level and are either directly under the county organization or operate independent of the county, sometimes as a branch of state government. The global COVID-19 pandemic has put a new focus on public health and the agencies that are responsible for helping to protect people. This section will focus on three issues: the need for a close cooperative relationship with public health officials, mental health and performance measurement.

The pandemic has demonstrated the critical importance of public health. Whether it is to implement public health precautions or assist in the vaccination of residents, it is in the vital interest of local governments to have a strong, cooperative relationship with public health officials and agencies. The time to develop and solidify that relationship is certainly well before disaster strikes.

The importance in improving mental health services for the community was emphasized in an earlier chapter. Cities and counties need to partner with public health agencies to support this cause. While mental health responsibilities may lie with an agency other than the public health department, they still play a significant role in it for the community through their closely aligned services and linkage with mentally ill patients.

The performance measures for cities and counties need to include outcomes that are not under their control or even principal influence. Where cities do not play the major role in achieving an outcome, they need to work with those who are most responsible and establish an appropriate outcome. For instance, the Newport News outcome–based performance measurement system contained a measure that is related to community public health.

Employee health care

Not only is the cost of employee health care a large issue for local governments but the amount of lost productivity due to ill employees is also a significant loss. The good news is that there are some steps that managers can take to reduce health care cost and absenteeism. From personal experience, there are two important initiatives that can really make a difference: an employee health clinic and a wellness program. As in some locations, the City of Greenville had a health clinic that provided some basic health screening and treatment. Every employee could get an annual physical exam, including a blood workup for no charge. This was tremendously valuable in identifying employee health problems much earlier than they would have otherwise been detected. I am convinced that this program actually saved the life of at least one employee and, undoubtedly more, during my tenure with the city. During an annual exam, the doctor identified a major issue and sent the employee to the hospital where they discovered a condition that would have been fatal in a relatively short period of time.

In Greenville as well as Newport News, we instituted wellness programs that made a major difference in employee health and insurance premiums. After the first year of operation in Greenville, we did not have any increase in the health insurance premiums despite others experiencing well into double-digit increases.

There are many elements to wellness programs that can be valuable. Three that I have found to be most helpful are health assessments, reimbursement for health club memberships and exercise equipment and a lower insurance premium for nonsmokers. The health assessments we used in Greenville and Newport News were voluntary. We paid an incentive to participate in the process. In Newport News, those who did a blood test (at city cost) and completed a health assessment received a $50 charge card. Those who also did a follow-up call with a nurse to go through their assessment received another $50 gift card. The incentive did help immensely in getting a good response, well over what other organizations have experienced without an incentive. We know from follow-ups that many people did work to address health issues that were identified.

In several places I managed, we provided funding for the purchase of exercise equipment or gym memberships. The funding came through allowing people to cash in sick time to pay for these items or a reimbursement based on sign up and usage. These steps were taken along with other activities such as in-house fitness classes provided by the city, smoking cessation classes or weight loss programs. All these programs were well utilized.

In several locations, I initiated a reduction in premium for those who committed to refrain from smoking. This was also very well utilized and provided sufficient incentive for many people to quit smoking for good.

This chapter on health care has demonstrated a value of working with other agencies to accomplish city objectives. The next chapter about intergovernmental relationships will take this much further.

11 Intergovernmental relations

All local government managers know that there are many factors affecting what happens in a city or a county that are beyond the control of their organization. Even within the governmental sphere, the actions of the federal and state governments have a tremendous influence on what a city can and cannot do. This is true for the ability to raise funds locally, the amount of public financial support provided outside localities, the regulations that are imposed and the way they operate. This chapter explores some of the major dimensions that managers deal with relating to other levels of government and some strategies that managers should pursue to effectively navigate the challenges and take advantage of the benefits of their state and the federal governments. This will include a look at both the regulations and funding at the regional, state and federal levels.

Federal government, the stick

The federal government carrot and stick exert a tremendous influence on the local government. I must preface my remarks that there is tremendous value in not only the carrot of funding provided for certain programs but also the stick of regulations that have been critical in improving our air and water quality and reducing urban flooding in addition to many other benefits.

Let's begin with the stick they wield, the regulations that are critical. It has already been mentioned that the Clean Water Act has provided a regulatory framework to ensure that wastewater is treated to a high level of quality and to reduce the negative impact of discharges to water bodies. Those regulations have sometimes presented unique challenges to the local government in which managers must become involved. I remember very well that in getting approval for one wastewater plant discharge when I was working for Hillsborough County, Florida, we

DOI: 10.4324/9781003262756-12

needed to show that not only was the quality of water not going to nega-
tively affect the water body but also the quantity was not going to create
problems either. This was because the outfall was going into a swampy
area and the regulatory authority was concerned that the discharge
would increase the water level to the point where the waterline would be
higher on some trees and affect their health and viability. This resulted
in paying a visit to the swamp where the discharge was occurring and
wading through it with hip waders to look at the water levels. As I did
that, I tried not to think of all the creatures lurking just beneath the
water level. We were successful in getting the permit approved but would
not have been without the visit to the swamp. The message here is as it
has been for other issues—there are times when a manager must get very
engaged in an issue and take an unusual approach to resolving concerns.

Another example involving wastewater regulations will help further
illustrate this point. When I first arrived as the Newport News City
Manager, the HRSD was in the process of studying a restructuring of
the roles for providing wastewater collection and treatment. At that
time, the cities and counties in the region had the responsibility for the
local collection system and HRSD was responsible for the major sewer
lines and the treatment and discharge of the wastewater. The region was
under a federal consent decree and state consent order for the quality of
the discharge into the Chesapeake Bay, a specially protected water body.
The plan being proposed by the HRSD was that they would assume
responsibility for the entire wastewater system operations and take over
the local government systems. This plan was being advanced because
they reasoned that by looking at the entire system, the improvements
to the discharges could be handled regionally and save a tremendous
amount of money in the process. The key improvements that needed
to occur with the local systems were reductions in the infiltration and
inflow.

The cities and counties had significant concerns because they would
lose the local autonomy on permitting connections to their systems as
well as the responsiveness they could provide for maintenance and
repairs. There were also significant impacts to the employees who would
either become employees of HRSD or lose their jobs. For example,
many of the Newport News employees were in a different retirement
system from HRSD, and they would lose much of the benefit of this
system if they had to switch to another one.

It is clear to me that the cities and counties were going to be solidly
against the proposal and the possible benefits of consolidation would
be lost. I talked to the HRSD executive director about an alternate
approach. My idea was to entrust to the HRSD the plan and to do all

the needed improvements on a regional basis. They would decide what improvements would need to be made to the local systems and the cities and counties would still maintain the local control of the individual collection systems. I told him I felt that the local governments would accept this and promised to help rally them behind this approach. I had already run this by the managers of some of the key cities to see if they would be open to this idea. While he told me that he was not ready to accept this idea, a week later he proposed this approach and it was indeed adopted by the region. There are times when a manager needs to be not only engaged but also very proactive in seeking solutions that involve agencies and authorities beyond their own local government.

The federal government has a very significant role in regulating air quality as I introduced in an earlier chapter. As explained previously, the regional organization for the Phoenix area, the Maricopa Association of Governments (MAG), had the responsibility for air quality planning. While we were in nonattainment status for ozone, carbon dioxide and particulates, we had developed plans that were approved by the EPA that showed the steps we would take to come into compliance with the allowed levels of these pollutants. Areas that are not in compliance with the standards must have an approved plan to continue to build improvements to their transportation system.

In 2000, a challenge by the Environmental Defense Fund (EDF) to the method that EPA was using in approving the regional air quality improvement plans was successful. This court decision had the effect of negating the approval of all the regional air quality improvement plans in the country and thereby causing a halt to all the transportation projects in many places. The Phoenix region was included in this group. However, we very quickly made changes to our plan to address the issues that had been raised by the EDF. Even with these changes, the federal authorities were going to consider our plan out of compliance and shut down our transportation construction program. We were in the process of the major construction of our regional freeway system.

I felt that reversing this could only be done by quickly elevating our appeal to the highest level of the agencies involved. This meant seeking the concurrence of the EPA Region Nine office, the Federal Highway Administration (FHWA) and the US Justice Department. We quickly met with the regional administrators of these offices, including flying to San Francisco to meet with the EPA. By carrying our case directly to high-level decision-makers, we were able to get the decision reversed and continue uninterrupted with our transportation improvements. Unfortunately, many major urban areas experienced a significant period of time with their programs shut down.

This story is told to emphasize the importance of being engaged on an issue, taking quick action when it is required and not being intimated by the federal bureaucracy. In addition, in critical situations, elevating an issue early and to the highest level where decisions are made and administrators sometimes see the bigger picture more clearly can make the difference between success and failure. If we had worked through the system from level to level up the hierarchy, we would have not been successful; there was simply no time to follow that process.

Federal government, the carrot

The complexities that are encountered in obtaining federal funding can be every bit as complicated and, at times, convoluted as federal regulations. The biggest lesson here is like the lottery—if you don't play, you can't win. Your city or county may not strike it rich, but the financial rewards for participating can make significant differences in a community. Although the rules of the game have changed a lot over the years and they will continue to change, it just means that managers need to keep up with the times.

My first successful experience came when I was a Senior Assistant County Administrator in Hillsborough County. In order to be effective, we decided to hire a lobbyist to assist in our effort to obtain federal funding. While there certainly is some cost involved, I learned early on how critical they can be to the process. We paid less than $100,000 for the contract and were successful in obtaining a $40 million dollar earmark for improvements to I-4. I was engaged in going to Washington to sell the proposal to our local Congressional leaders.

A second critical lesson is you must go to DC and meet with the decision-makers. You can't just catch them when they are in the home district. Meeting them in their office makes all the difference. Additionally, you need to go with a specific ask and it needs to be something they can help you to obtain. Whenever I subsequently met with Senators and Congressmen, which would include those in Minnesota, Arizona, South Carolina and Virginia, I always went with some specific requests that they could act on and limited it to no more than four items. I have found that the best time to meet with the Senators and Congressmen is not during the time when professional groups have their Washington, DC, conferences but at least two weeks before, when you have a better chance for a small group meeting. Lobbyists can be most helpful in setting up those meetings; that is a significant part of their value. They work hard to develop and maintain a good working relationship with the congressional staffs.

The funding for I-4 was obtained at a time when the earmarking process was alive and well. As part of the budget process, you could get specific appropriations written into the budget. This was not always easy. Earlier, I mentioned obtaining funding approval for the light rail system start in Phoenix. While we were seeking to obtain the federal funding, we were greatly challenged by the then Senator John McCain who was adamantly opposed to the earmarking process. We were successful in simply neutralizing him by getting him to agree to not object to our request and working on the other members of our delegation to actively support the effort. While working in South Carolina, I ran up against the same challenge with Senator Jim DeMint. However, we did achieve a greater than seven million dollar earmark for a city road improvement, his very last earmark. After that, he refused to participate in the process and did not run again for his senate position.

While earmarks became a thing of the past, they are currently being resurrected in a more restrained fashion. In addition, grants are alive and well, although the processes can be extremely competitive. However, they can be tremendously helpful. I told the story in my prior book about obtaining a $20 million dollar grant for a sludge facility at the very end of the wastewater grant program. Shortly after that, it was turned into a loan program. We met the deadline by offering a 10% bonus to the designer if he could meet a very compressed design schedule. I also described a major renovation project that provided the City of Greenville an updated convention facility with the cobbling together of state and federal grants. In that case, we were able to obtain federal funding because it could be used as an emergency shelter. Part of the lesson learned was that there are many different ways to obtain funding that may not be apparent but which deep searches can uncover. As I indicated before, managers need to be ever watchful for the latest developments on the state and federal levels. With the latest effort to do a large federally funded infrastructure program, it certainly appears that grants for water and wastewater projects will be revived.

Another grant process for Greenville yields some added lessons. The city had successfully completed a Hope VI grant for redeveloping a city neighborhood. Although the program was very competitive and the city had already received one, we were successful in receiving a second grant. Our success was principally due to the performance on the first grant and having a good relationship with the federal decision-makers. We also took a small delegation to Washington to meet with them. Having the city manager along demonstrated the commitment of the city to perform with this second grant and show the priority we attached to it.

It is very clear that one of the keys to successfully obtaining federal money is having a lobbyist who is familiar with the subject matter and has a good working relationship with the congressman and senators from your state. The earmark we received for I-4 improvements was greatly assisted by a member of the lobbying firm that had been the staff director of the House Public Works Committee. In obtaining the Hope VI grant, we were assisted by someone who had great relationships with HUD. While firms generally tilt toward one political party or the other, it is important to select a firm that has good relationships with both parties. In every instance where my city or county hired a lobbyist firm, the amount of money generated with their assistance was paid back many times the federal funding received.

Federal committees

While participating in various extracurricular activities that are beyond the job description of a city manager can be time consuming and add extra hours to the already busy day, they can be rewarding not only individually but also to the organization and community as well as to the profession. In my first book, I discussed the value of participating in volunteer activities in the community, especially nonprofits and charitable fund raising. Here, I would like to discuss taking part in activities on a national level.

While serving as the MAG executive director, I was appointed by the International City/County Management Association (ICMA) as their representative to the US Commerce Secretary's Census Advisory Committee. I served as their representative for seven years. This committee provided advice on the policies and procedures for carrying out the census. I was on the committee during the lead up and execution of the 2000 census. This involved making several trips each year (up to as many as seven in one year) to Washington to meet with census officials. Even though the Census Bureau paid all expenses, this did take time away from my job. This was minimized quite a bit by working throughout the long plane ride back and forth and we only met for at most two days. It was a bit of a challenge with the two- or three-hour time difference between Arizona and DC (Arizona does not go on daylight saving time, so there is a three-hour difference for more than half the year). At times, the meetings would start at 7:00 AM eastern, 4:00 AM in Arizona.

I would like to think that my contributions helped the country to conduct a better census. I do know that they certainly helped the Phoenix region get a capture more of its total number of residents. The region was and still is a rapidly growing place. During the late 1990s, the metropolitan area was adding more than 100,000 new residents a year. That made it particularly difficult for the Census Bureau to maintain an up-to-date address file for all the newcomers. In fact, the initial Census Bureau procedures were using an address file about a year old. This would have missed mailing out census forms to households—to about 100,000 people. At the time, the generally accepted rule of thumb was that each additional person counted resulted in an additional $10,000 of federal funding going to the state. Even if the bureau was able to pick up a lot of the new residents, the state still stood to lose a lot in federal revenue. Since the number of US House of Representatives is based on population, the state could also possibly have lost an extra member.

To address this, I pressed the Census Bureau to do another update of the address file close to the time of the census. This was accepted, and high-growth areas around the country, like Phoenix, were able to have a more inclusive accounting of their residents. Besides this being a rewarding experience, it added significant value to the region I served.

All the ICMA committees I served on brought personal reward as well as substantial professional development through the interaction with other professionals who provided their valuable insight to the profession and gave me great ideas to implement back home. One of the most interesting and valuable benefits was serving as ICMA's representative to the Commission on Fire Accreditation International. After reviewing many applications for the accreditation of fire departments around the country and beyond, it was even more obvious to me why the public has such a high regard for the fire service. As an aside, it was ironic that I reviewed the application of a city I had previously work for.

State control of local government

While the state where a local government is located does make a difference in the amount of control it has over local affairs, all state governments exert a great deal of control over their operations. Having been a manager for localities in ten different states, I can say that the relationship between the state government and the cities and counties is always a challenge. State law generally determines the types of taxes and fees that localities can levy and the rules for how they levy them. States also control a significant amount of revenue that is provided to cities and towns for their operations. Because of this, local governments must be active in supporting their positions to the state legislatures and develop and maintain a close working relationship with the departments of the state. States also often dictate the ways in which cities and counties control their planning and land use.

One example of obtaining state funding will help drive home the importance of the state's control of the purse strings. When I assumed the Newport News City Manager position (a lot of stories have started out this way, haven't they), the city had a project to build an inter-modal transportation facility. This facility would combine an Amtrak station, interstate and regional bus stops and link to the Newport News/Williamsburg Airport. The original cost of the project had ballooned, for a number of reasons, and the city found itself short of $20 million of the $40 million price tag. I quickly developed a good professional relationship with the head of the State's Department of Public Transportation. The staff worked hard to develop a case for the value and benefit of the project. We also worked on others at the regional level to support the project. We were able to obtain approximately $20 million in extra funding from the state and make the project viable.

The Greenville Convention Center renovation I previously mentioned not only benefited from federal funding but we also received a state grant of seven million dollars for the project. I could relate many stories of the critical value of state funding. As in many other lessons, this is another example in which a manager needs to be directly involved. The manager needs to work to build relationships with both the administrative and legislative arms of the state. I have previously been on a first-name basis with five different governors (they called me Jim, I called them by their first name, Governor...).

Regional governance

Having managed cities and counties as well as serving as the executive director of a regional council of governments, in ten different states, I have seen a wide variety of approaches to regional governance. I also served as a consultant to study a regional council and make recommendations on whether to overhaul or disband the agency. Of course, we do not have true regional government in this country. Consolidated city and county operations like Metro Nashville where I began my career do unite cities in a county but does not capture the remainder of the urban region. One of the agencies that probably comes the closest is the Metropolitan Council (Metro Council) serving the seven counties (including Hennepin County) making up the Minneapolis–St. Paul metro area. The Metro Council provides not only the planning function for the region but also the operation of the transit system and the major wastewater system components and a regional parks and trails system.

In addition to this regional government, the Twin Cities also has a unique tax sharing program, generally referred to as the Fiscal Disparities Program. This program, which the legislature established, redistributes 40% of the amount of the increase in the commercial industrial property tax base to the cities and counties based on a formula that seeks to balance the wealth among the cities and counties. Because Hennepin County had a relatively high property tax base, as I started the budget for Hennepin County each year, I generally had to account for a redistribution of around $75 million of revenue to other localities. This program has indeed somewhat evened out the disparities of the tax bases. The problem is that it only looks at revenue and not the need for expenditures. For instance, while it is indeed true that Hennepin County has a very strong tax base, it also has many needs that are disproportionate to other locations. One of these is the social welfare program costs, which is by far the largest in the state. However, even with this issue and the challenge it presents to Hennepin County, there are some clear benefits to this program.

Despite advantages that the Metro Council and Fiscal Disparities Program may bring to the Twin Cities, it is most unlikely that similar programs will be instituted in many other programs in this country. In fact, most often, cities and counties put up a great deal of resistance to any regional control. However, there are programs, such as transportation planning, that must be done on a regional level according to federal law and there are great examples of cooperation among localities in a region. Groups of cities and counties have banded together to provide services on a regional level that can take advantage of economies of scale and accomplish things that could not be done just within a city or county. Certainly, HRSD is an example of that as well as the regional jail facilities in the Hampton Roads area, like many others around the country.

The remaining portion of this chapter will focus on the structure of regional agencies and some recommendations for effective organizations. Most regional agencies generally take the form of a council of governments, an association formed by the cities and counties in a metropolitan area. Sometimes, that body serves as the Transportation Planning Organization (TPO) as in MAG, but sometimes, there is a different agency designated to perform this function. Generally, all the local governments in an area are members of the agency, but, in some instances, a city or county may have opted out for one reason or another. These bodies are generally governed by a council made up of all the cities and counties. In some instances, other members may be part of the council, such as with MAG where the state transportation commission has a member on the board.

In order to deal with the difference in the size of the member organizations, many regions provide for some form of proportional representation, allotting the number of members for each jurisdiction based on their population. As one might expect, that can lead to very large councils. Others handle the equity of different size cities and counties by employing a weighted vote—that is, giving each locality a number of votes based on their populations. Often, that weighted vote is only used when asked for one or more members, as most votes are generally supported by all, if not almost all, the members.

The members of a regional council are generally designated or appointed elected officials from each of the member agencies. Sometimes, the mayors are the designated member, and other times, each city or county council will appoint someone to serve for the term of a year. There are some occasions when a nonelected official may be designated to serve on the regional governing body. This is the situation with the Hampton Roads Regional Planning District Commission (HRPDC), where the city and county managers serve as members along with the mayor and some council members who make up the proportional representation.

My first recommendation dealing with regional governing bodies is to avoid city and county managers serving on the governing body alongside elected officials. In addition to this being a very awkward situation, it puts the manager in a very difficult position. As a member, the manager really needs to vote on issues based on what they think is best for the region. So what happens when their votes would be counter to what the mayor or council members who represent their city would like to see happen? It becomes even deicer when the mayor and any council member sitting on the regional governing body disagree on a vote and the manager ends up having to, in essence, pick a side. Not a career enhancing move. In addition, this changes the role of the manager from one of giving advice to one of deciding an outcome alongside their boss. The more appropriate role is for the manager to provide recommendations for the elected officials who sit on the regional council.

I was presented with a bit of a similar circumstance when I served on the board of the Newport News/Williamsburg Airport Authority alongside a council member from my city. However, the nature of the issues was quite different, and there was never an occasion that represented a conflict between the position I took and that of the council member.

I attempted to change the governing body structure for HRPDC when serving as the Newport News City Manager. At the time, I was also serving as the Chair of the Hampton Roads City and County Managers. The proposal that the group of managers recommended to the regional council was to eliminate the managers from the council and formally recognize a body of the city and county managers to make recommendations to the council on issues that the region faced. The recommendation also included changing from a proportional represen-tation to a single representative for each member agency and employ weighted voting if requested by a member. This proposal was intended to address not only the problem of the managers sitting on the council but also the very large size of the council, over 40 members.

It appeared initially that the regional council was very open to the proposal. However, when some of the council members, particularly from the largest city, Virginia Beach, heard that they would no longer be on the council, they were concerned. The real irony is that these members never attended the meetings, even when there were relatively controversial issues. Also, the city would have had more voting power with the weighted vote than the existing proportional representation. We all know that change is never easy. The proposal was not accepted due to the opposition of the biggest cities. I will also add that a couple of the managers expressed a concern with not being on the council because they would not be there to serve as a check on their mayor who might take a bad position. That seems like a pretty slippery slope for the manager. Of course, they did not share that position with their mayor.

MAG does have a management committee, which consists of all the city and county managers in the region, which meets monthly, prior to the regional council, and makes recommendations on each of the issues coming up on the regional council agenda. It is positioned to give expert and timely advice to the elected officials. It also serves as a terrific sounding board for the executive director on issues that are important to the region. This is a structure that I would recommend for regional councils.

As I indicated previously, in some instances the regional council serves as the TPO for the region. In other instances, it does not. In fact, in some instances the boundary of the regional council does not coin-cide with the boundary for the TPO. Both situations present issues for effective decision-making. It was emphasized earlier that it is important to do transportation planning in conjunction with land use planning and the planning for other public infrastructure. Having a separate regional body to solely do transportation planning only makes it more difficult to have a coordinated approach.

Even though, at times, there is a separate governing body for the trans-portation decision-making and all other regional actions, both bodies may be served by the same staff. This is the case with the HRPDC, whose staff also serves the Hampton Roads Regional Transportation Planning Organization (HRTPO). In addition, the HRTPO meets immediately following the HRPDC to minimize the travel time for the members. While there still is some confusion created, it is better than two separate organizations served by two separate staffs.

Unfortunately for Hampton Roads, the situation has been made more complicated by local and state politics. The state passed special legislation that provides additional transportation funding for the Hampton Roads area. In the process of determining how decisions would be made for this revenue stream, the state general assembly and transportation commissioner wanted to exert their control on how the money would be spent. So instead of giving the spending authority to the already existing TPO, they created yet another regional organization in which the transportation commissioner was engaged to allocate the available money. Thus, there are now three regional agencies involved in decision-making. Even though, yet again, some of the same local leaders are involved in all three boards, it makes for a very disjointed process. And this time, they even created a new staff entity to advise this additional board.

In the discussions of various aspects of city and county issues, we have touched on the importance of technology. However, since automation is so critical, the next chapter is devoted entirely to this subject.

12 Technology

City and county managers certainly do not need the skills of a computer programmer. However, they definitely not only need to understand how to use a computer and do research over the internet but also need to be current in the ways in which computer technology can be applied to the functions of their organization. Clearly, that is no easy task with the rapidly changing world of advancing automation. I once asked my organization to come up with a technology plan for the next five years knowing that it would not take five years for that plan to be out of date. Indeed, we moved beyond it in 18 months. A local government can be on the cutting edge of computer technology at one point and not too much later be left behind without a constant refresh. When I arrived in 1993 as the Hennepin County Administrator, the county was resting on its laurels of leading the way in innovative technology with its two massive mainframe computers that ran virtually all the applications for the county. Thousands of employees logged into these massive mainframes with their dumb terminals (no computing capacity). Over the next few years, there was a shift away from this model to a system of networked personal computers. The information technology (IT) staff loved those big boxes and resisted changing to a new model. I believe that this resistance to adopting a new model held the county back in being as effective as it could have been. This chapter will examine some technology issues for city operations and budgeting concerns as well as technology issues for the community.

There are obviously multitudes of issues for managers to be up-to-date with automation and many, many things to consider. However, I would like to focus on five items in this section.

- Cloud computing
- Security
- Automating functions

DOI: 10.4324/9781003262756-13

- Budgeting for automation
- Community internet access

Cloud computing

I know many organizations, for various reasons, have resisted the transformation from their onsite hardware, software and data storage to benefiting from cloud computing services. While everyone has surely heard the term *cloud computing*, some may not be as familiar as others about what it is exactly. Wikipedia says that Wikipedia (n.d.) says that:

> Cloud computing is the on-demand availability of computer system resources, especially data storage (cloud storage) and computing power without direct active management by the user.

Some mistrust the reliability and security of a system that they do not personally control. However, there are significant advantages of this approach for local governments. From a governmental perspective, I believe that the principal benefits are the following:

- Flexibility/nimbleness
- Less up-front investment
- Virtually limitless capacity
- Enhanced security

When the systems that a city uses are tied to their physical hardware and the software they run, it is more difficult to makes changes in those systems than if they are supported by cloud technology, which provides greater flexibility. Since cloud computing requires less hardware owned by the locality, there is less capital cost and investment. Cloud technology is backed up by large systems that can absorb the requirements of local users and the user is not limited by the amount of computing capacity or storage that the locality may have in its system. The providers of cloud computing have very sophisticated security systems that protect the data better than local governments can for their own systems. While some may fear the breaches of these large systems, their own networks are truly more vulnerable.

Security

If the fear of information getting into the hands of computer hackers was not already enough of a concern, the advent of ransomware and the demands of extortionists, the cost to repair damage and the downtime are certainly enough to give managers sleepless nights. Anyone not concerned just does not understand their vulnerabilities. When I started as the Newport News City Manager, I was worried about our system security. The IT staff had previously recommended an assessment of the system vulnerability, but the cost of a consultant had not been approved. I felt that it was essential to do a review, and we hired a consultant very skilled in computer network security. While it was very sensitive at the time, I can now more freely say that they found 3,000 different ways that someone could break into our "secure system." We plugged those holes, but it is a constant challenge to ensure system security. All local governments should have a penetration test done periodically to know where the weaknesses are and take action to address them. I strongly recommend that the local government should contract with an outside expert. I know that many of the larger and more sophisticated entities may believe that they have it covered with their IT staff. While the staff may have great skills, they are still members of the locality's organization and see the issues through the lens of the city. Having a fresh set of eyes from the outside that have seen many different systems can be invaluable. I should disclose that I have been involved in doing some consultation with Elliott Davis, my previous firm that has an extensive cyber security practice. However, I became involved principally to help bring a needed service to local governments. This is money very well spent.

Despite the tremendous threat that has existed for quite a number of years, both public and private sector leaders and the public in general have been too slow to realize the tremendous threat that exists from cyberattacks. The ransomware attack on the Colonial Pipeline in May 2021 demonstrated the vulnerability of our infrastructure and the economic damage that can be created. While the hacker's main stated interest is in making money, it is a serious form of modern warfare.

Automating functions

In general terms, any local government that does not already have a plan for going to a paperless operation for all their functions needs to develop one. We started this process in Newport News more than five years ago. It indeed takes a long time to get there. In reality, cities will need to maintain some ability for residents to continue to work with paper, but the overwhelming number of functions can be automated. The savings in staff time and gained efficiencies will be tremendous. Additionally, there will be a large benefit for the environment. This does require an investment to digitize paper records and obtain systems for automated operations, but the long-term savings will justify the near-term cost.

It is particularly critical to automate some very important functions: the land use and building permitting system, property records and utility meter reading. There are already excellent software programs available to computerize the processing of requests for land use changes, subdivision approval and building permit application and inspection. These allow the staff to not only communicate better with one another but also enhance the information available for the applicant. This automation will also assist in the evaluation of the performance of the system. These systems allow for the electronic submission of plan documents. This may require substantial hardware upgrades, but there are great efficiencies with the ability to transfer documents not only to and from the public but also from staff member to staff member.

There are also systems available for automating property records. Automating this function is a huge service to the public. With this automation, there are some significant policy issues. Localities will need to decide what level of access the public will be provided. The biggest decision is whether to provide access to ownership information to all members of the public. I believe that this level of access certainly makes sense especially given the wide availability of information from many sources.

There are also very large benefits for Advanced Metering Infrastructure (AMI) where there is an ability to not only read a utility meter remotely but also send instructions to the meter. This AMI technology is now being installed in cities in many parts of this country. Electric companies are also using this technology. While the applications of the same systems could be applied to other functions, the industry providing the hardware and software has not responded to the potential benefit of using the system for added functions and has focused on single uses. Those envisioning "smart cities" see the possibilities of using similar technology to have sensors to allow public works crews to know when a bridge may have ice on it or when a public trash can needs to be emptied or even let the public know where available parking is located. While cities are implementing AMI, the industry leaders need to be examining ways to broaden the technology applications in order to improve operations.

Budgeting for automation

In the 37 years I was engaged in public sector management, I never saw a time when there was plenty of money to go around and meet all the needs of a city or county. So competition is always tough. However, managers need to establish a priority to fund computer automation. There needs to be sufficient funds for technology equipment refresh in the budget every year. There needs to be money for new system development as well as risk assessment. If this is not something valued by a city or county council, there are efficiency studies that can be done that demonstrate the value in improved productivity that investment in technology brings. This is especially true in times of cutbacks. Increased efficiencies through technology can provide avenues to save valuable resources.

As long as technology has been around, there have been internal debates of whether to budget for hardware and software in the operating user department or centrally in an IT department. One of the main arguments for budgeting in the operating departments is that it forces the department to more carefully evaluate the need for the equipment and services if they have to balance the costs with all the competing demands. Among the arguments for budgeting in a central IT department is the enhanced control for the consistency and quality of the purchasing decisions. It seems to me the answer is somewhere in the middle. The IT department needs to set standards for the devices that can be purchased, so there is consistency across the organization. In addition, there are some devices that are probably best budgeted at the department level, such as mobile phones. Devices such as these are items the department will want to prioritize as important for their staff. Of course, there also needs to be some standards set on who can get a mobile phone. Additionally, there are some costs that are best budgeted within the IT department, such as technology refresh. It is unlikely that departments will sufficiently understand the importance of hardware replacement. Also, expenditures for systems that bridge many departments ought to be budgeted centrally.

Community internet access

While the disparity of the availability of internet access across the country has been a significant issue for many years, the COVID-19 pandemic has highlighted the inequities and social justice issues that it presents. Consistent with Chapter 1, this needs to be a priority for local governments. It also needs to be a priority for the state and federal governments as well because addressing this issue can be beyond the resources that cities and counties can realistically bring to the table. In addition, localities in some states are constrained by state and federal law on what they can require private broadband companies to do. Even if that is the case, they can work with them to provide some subsidies for extending services. Some states also restrict the broadband services that a city might provide, which would be in competition with the private sector.

However, there are some solutions that cities can pursue, like providing Wi-Fi hot spots in underserved areas and helping to encourage private companies to extend broadband to underserved areas. While Wi-Fi hot spots are not the long-term solution to internet access, their use in urban areas with relatively high densities of underserved can be effective. While localities are constrained by state and federal law on what they can require private broadband companies to do, they can work with them to provide some subsidies for extending services.

Most of the issues covered thus far in this book require some engagement with the public, and there is always an affirmative responsibility for the cities and counties to inform the public of their actions. The next chapter gets into these issues and strategies for effectively engaging with the public.

Reference

Wikipedia. n.d. 2021. "Cloud Computing". Accessed August 20. https://en.wikipedia.org/wiki/Cloud_computing

13 Public engagement

Engaging citizens in a substantive way in all but the most controversial issues involving the local government has always been a challenge. I can remember quite a number of public hearings on the annual budget for cities or counties that I managed when less than a handful of residents showed up to testify. Even then, it was only the frequent flyers who became largely involved to see themselves on television. As jaded as that may sound to some, it is really not meant to be. People lead busy lives and have many obligations and if they see that something is not broken, they are not inclined to spend much of their limited time with family to come to a night meeting, sometimes in bad weather. (Even as hardy as the people are in Minnesota, the weather can be treacherous.) So how does a city best engage its citizens in a meaningful way? After all, it **is** their community's government. This chapter will explore how best to inform and engage citizens. But first, the citizen dynamic that has developed, especially over the past several years, must be examined.

Examining the general outlook of citizens toward their government and how they conduct themselves, I believe that there is substantial difference today than when I started in public administration in the late 1970s. The current lack of civility is, frankly, very disturbing. This lack of civility is across the board with citizens as well as elected officials. My personal view, which has been echoed by many others, is that certainly one of the leading causes is a lack of trust of the federal government and frustration with the inability of the elected leaders to effectively govern and the animosity that they show to one another. When the elected leaders they voted for show rancor to the other side, they tend to emulate that behavior. In most states, that same dynamic is at play and the citizens reflect the incivility shown at that level as well.

Of course, all this has been stoked not only by social media but also by purported television "news" that operates more as opinionated broadcasts. Here is where I can take a bit more license as a **former**

DOI: 10.4324/9781003262756-14

manager. It is very clear that the right-wing media, especially, has played more than a bit fast and loose with the facts. But that is really a bit irrelevant for the point. This level of angst that is mostly generated at a national and, to some extent, state level certainly flows down to the local level. Since the local level is the closest to the people and is the easiest for people to access, this current lack of civility often gets felt at the city and county levels. This sometimes translates to a lack of trust in elected and appointed officials. Of course, this is not always the case, as there are a lot of citizens who truly appreciate the local services provided and do show respect for the employees. However, those who do not can be downright nasty.

Another cause of this anger and incivility can be a lack of understanding of the process and how decisions are made, which leads to a level of mistrust. This is mentioned separately because there are definitely some positive steps that can be taken to address this.

Conducting council meetings

So, indeed, how should managers respond to this civility challenge? I will focus on the dynamic in meetings first. The role of the mayor or chair of the board is vitally important. There must be clear standards of conduct that spell out what is acceptable and what is not acceptable. This goes for council members as well as members of the public. I would add that staff should obviously be included, but they are rarely the instigators but most often the recipient of attacks. No personal attacks of any kind should be allowed. If someone starts to violate this tenant, they need to be stopped and not allowed to continue. You just cannot allow this to go on at all and must intervene.

In conducting meetings, some councils slide into a bit more informal procedures. This can lead to bad behavior and should be avoided. For instance, by never allowing comments from the audience, you help control the unacceptable outbursts that can happen with a controversial issue. In addition, the amount of back and forth between a citizen and the council or staff must be minimized. It is fine for the council to ask a citizen questions, but the best protocol is for the citizen getting up to the podium to speak and being allowed to make their point; the council ask any questions and then the citizen must **sit down**. Much of the antagonistic behavior can be eliminated by preventing an escalating "dialog" between the parties. Council members asking questions to solicit information needs to be carefully controlled. More often than not, a council member will be asking a citizen questions to attempt to lead the citizen to make a point for the council member.

Staff can play a key role in enhancing the process and not adding to the tension. Information should be presented in a straightforward fashion, designed to be clear and easy to understand. The staff also needs to present and answer any questions but avoid unnecessary time at the podium engaging the council or citizens. One of the biggest coaching roles I played with department directors is to make sure they knew when to sit down. This is especially true if there is aggressive questioning by a council member. It is the manager who needs to absorb the brunt of a council member's aggressive behavior, not the department director.

Good relationships between the council and staff are critical. When the council starts to abuse staff, they sometimes want to later bad mouth the council member. The manager must stop this. They are the elected official, and staff cannot object to the way council members conduct themselves. It is up to the manager to address it with the council member. That is best done in a one-on-one meeting unless it is so out of line that something needs to be said at the meeting. This should be only on the rarest of occasions.

It should go without saying that the decorum of board members toward one another is critically important. Everyone takes their cues from that, and they demonstrate what is acceptable and not acceptable. They set the tone.

Informing and engaging citizens

Some words in government and the media become so overused they almost lose their meaning. I almost cringe when I see the word *transparency* used in so many different ways. However, it is a critically important concept when talking about engaging citizens. I will once again look to Wikipedia for a working definition. It says that transparency "… is operating in such a way that it is easy for others to see what actions are performed. Transparency implies openness, communication and accountability." It seems to me, this captures an aspirational goal. Cities and counties obviously need to be open in what, how and why decisions are made. The communication with the public must be clear, understandable and timely.

When the transparency concept really started to be discussed extensively, part of the answer to financial transparency advocated by some was to have local governments, in essence, put their check ok online. Nothing could be more absurd than having a listing of hundreds and, in some cases, thousands of checks listed without some idea of what they were purchasing and how it was to be used. Not even a city manager could make heads or tails of that. Rather, putting online financial information in a form that allowed citizens to explore the expenditures by department and by major purpose, such as personnel, travel and training or equipment would tell the story much better. Companies developed software packages which did that in a very user-friendly way for citizens to manipulate and explore. A package we utilized in Newport News developed by OpenGov fit that purpose and was very well received and utilized by citizens.

I feel that type of approach should be the model. Information must be provided that gets to the heart of the matter and in an understandable way informs the community of what their local government is doing. I think a big part of this needs to be an outcome-based performance measurement system that describes the results of the city's actions and services across the organization. In the City of Newport News, we developed a series of 69 outcome measures. The results for each year were presented to the public in the annual state of the city and posted on the website.

As cities or counties develop measures to share with the community, they must be rigorous to focus on results not merely outputs. A manager may pride themselves on increasing the number of lane miles of roadway repaved each year, but that is a fairly meaningless measure if the city needed to pave twice the current number of lane miles in order to have better roadways conditions. The city needs to report on the condition of the pavement rather than the amount of repaving completed.

It is also essential to provide timely and accurate information to the news media and spend as much time as necessary in going through the information to ensure as accurate as possible reporting. Unfortunately, this is not enough. Even in the best of circumstances, the news media will not fully and accurately report the information that citizens need to know. The city needs to find ways to tell its own story. Using social media is certainly necessary and desirable. Hire people (they will probably need to be on the younger side) to work the social media scene. This will mean continually pushing out stories on Facebook or Twitter or other social media platforms. This effort must involve all departments and be comprehensive in nature.

A large percentage of cities and counties have gone to telecasting council meetings and/or live streaming them. The public pretty much expects that at this point. However, be sure to also make those meeting recordings available on a timely basis and provide detailed agendas well in advance of the meetings, as well as provide copies of minutes as close to their adoption as possible. I have been amazed at places that do not do that. With the technology that exists, cities and counties of any size can and must make live and recorded meetings available.

Additionally, taking great care in providing notice for executive sessions and the topics to be discussed is critical. And executive sessions need to be held only when they are absolutely necessary. Nothing will sow the seeds of distrust like citizens feeling that the council is conducting their major business in private, with no explanation to what is being done. As difficult as it is, managers must play a role in helping to coach councils on what can and cannot be discussed in an executive session. Managers can make sure that city attorneys are engaged in this effort as they are sometimes better positioned for the council to accept their guidance on this matter.

Newport News Now

Even with all these steps, I have found it necessary to do more to tell the city story. In Newport News, we started a **daily** electronic newsletter that went out to citizens. *Newport News Now* started with a list of 75,000 local email addresses. The newsletter was a single page with generally three stories told in a paragraph or two with hyperlinks to longer stories in some cases. The stories ranged from major projects to events in the city. I felt that it was essential that it be daily in order to set the expectation and consistency. It was amazing how quickly citizens embraced the newsletter and relied on the information it provided. We received wonderful feedback from the community. I was delighted that we had a vehicle to tell our story that exceeded the circulation of the daily newspaper. It is sometimes a litmus test for the value of an initiative that it survives after the manager who started it has departed. More than four years after I left the city, *Newport News Now* is still going strong.

Neighborhood engagement

In addition to engaging citizens on a community-wide basis, it is vital to be involved at a neighborhood level. In my earlier book, I described the community outreach effort we took in Newport News when we started an annual marathon that ran through many city neighborhoods. Bringing the plan to the neighborhoods and institutions in those areas made all the difference for not only their acceptance of having the race disrupt their normal routines but also for their embracing and participating in the event. This went a long way in helping the race become a great success. This is another event that has continued to prosper after the city manager left.

Business community engagement

Just as it is important to reach out and inform citizens about the city, it is also critically important to engage with the business community. This means not only participating in business organizations like the local chamber of commerce, board of realtors and home builders but also attending business luncheons and dinners. Managers need to have the pulse of the business community and business leadership in the city need to know what the city is doing for them. In addition to the knowledge transfer, it is about building relationships. Those relationships can be extremely important when a manager needs to know how the business community may respond to a proposal that will affect them or when the manager needs to give them a heads-up and explain an action with which they disagree.

Community organizations

I am a great believer in managers being involved with the philanthropic and nonprofit social service providers. In addition to providing a link with the city, my service to United Way organizations, particularly with fundraising activity, was very rewarding. It also certainly helped the community know that my heart was in it with them.

This and previous chapters have certainly covered a lot of ground. The final chapter will provide some concluding thoughts.

14 Conclusion

While the previous chapters in this book covered only the approaches to the most critical issues for managers, those issues were enough to fill up an entire book. Clearly, there is a lot on the plate of every city and county manager. And it certainly appears that plate will stay full for this decade and beyond. In addition, the plate has many volatile and controversial offerings. Many will require managers to make courageous recommendations to councils. These recommendations will need to be in the interest of the community but may be uncomfortable for city councils. The challenges may require doing things differently from they have done before. They may require pushing new ideas and solutions to intractable problems.

The status quo is not an option when one considers the needs for promoting social justice and police reform as well as addressing socio-economic disparities. It is not an option since global warming continues to melt massive sheets of ice in the artic regions and threaten not only coastal cities around the world but also the earth's ecological balance. It is not an option when we see ever more open space being taken by sprawling development. It is not an option as the rapid increases in housing costs, mental illness and drug addiction push more people into homelessness. It is not an option with the crisis faced by those without adequate health care. And it is not an option when the divisions in this country stoke insurrection and bloodshed.

Managers and other city leaders can and must make a difference. They must exhibit courage and fortitude to help chart a path toward equal treatment, equal access to a good quality of life and sustainability for our planet. While it is the council's responsibility for making policy decisions and adopting ordinances to govern, managers must clearly articulate the best path for a community and eloquently point out what is best for the locality. This will not always be easy for a manager whose council may want to be told something different and ignore the tough

DOI: 10.4324/9781003262756-15

realities and difficult choices. Managers need to do this even if it puts their positions at risk and sometimes it will.

Managers and other city leaders are in a position to make significant contribution to address the challenges of the 2020s. How they respond will be critical in making progress. It is not ok to just do the proscribed tasks of an administrator. Managers need to constantly be on the lookout for better ways of doing things and challenge the staff to do the same. Finding ways to address the challenges of today and tomorrow is where the real reward is for managers. Making a difference is indeed both the reason for the job and its reward.

Index

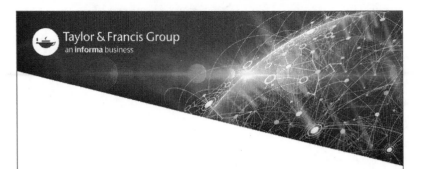